HILLS
— AND —
VALLEYS

A JOURNEY THROUGH HEALING AFTER AN AFFAIR

As Outlined by Psalm 34

A N N A H U E R T A

WESTBOW
PRESS®
A DIVISION OF THOMAS NELSON
& ZONDERVAN

WestBow Press books may be ordered through booksellers or by contacting:

WestBow Press
A Division of Thomas Nelson & Zondervan
1663 Liberty Drive
Bloomington, IN 47403
www.westbowpress.com
844-714-3454

ISBN: 978-1-6642-2177-2 (sc)
ISBN: 978-1-6642-2176-5 (e)

Library of Congress Control Number: 2021901937

Print information available on the last page.

WestBow Press rev. date: 05/07/2021

PREFACE

A few months after the affair and while I was still in deep mourning, wrought with hurt, and tormented by anger, the Lord spoke a blessing over me. Rather, He spoke it over you to me. In the midst of a women's Bible study and learning how God used the ugly, challenging, and painful things in our lives to bring glory to Himself and blessing to others, He told me that He intended to use my pain for good. I was intensely angry. I demanded, *Lord, nothing good can come of this*. Yet gently and tenderly, He kept pressing me until I relented. I agreed to allow Him to use my story to bless and minister to others, but I was still a long way from being happy about it.

The Holy Spirit took my willingness to obey and turned it into desire. I began looking for ways to bless others with my story and wondering in prayer what exactly *using it for good* would look like. Years later, the idea of writing a book came from a friend. I had no intention of putting my story on paper unless I ensured that the focus would be solely on Jesus. So I began praying over what kind of book to write.

It seemed that a Bible study was the only suitable option. I could think of nothing else that would give women the hope and the tools that they needed to heal other than taking them (you) straight to Jesus. After all, that was how I was healed. Praying, seeking, reading my Bible, and crying out to the Lord day and night, and day after day after day, was how I survived the darkest, most painful days of my life. Because it is a Bible study, this book is not designed to answer all your questions. My intent is to take you by the hand, lead you to Jesus, and teach you how to listen to Him for the answers to your questions.

If you do not have a personal relationship with Jesus and have never trusted Him with your heart and life, you are invited to pray with me and ask Him to be your King, Master, and Healer. Prayer is simply talking to your Creator and acknowledging that you have nothing without Him and come with nothing to offer. He has sent His only Son to die for you—to take away all your past failures, regrets, rebellion, and all that you have done to wound His heart. Jesus died a criminal's death in your place, and was raised from the dead so that your life and marriage can be raised to life along with Him. If you believe this, pray the following with me:

Father,

Thank You for sending Your Son, Jesus, to die for me. I believe that He is the only way to be set free of my failures and wrongs. I want to trust Him today to be my Healer and King. Please come into my life and make me wholly committed to You. Please use these next five weeks to show Yourself real to me and teach me how to respond to You in love and obedience. In the name of Jesus, Your Son, I ask these things. Amen.

ACKNOWLEDGMENTS

I want to thank my husband for his faithful support, encouragement, and patience, as I wrestled through these challenging and emotional lessons. I am continually grateful for you, your courage, and your drive to stick it out with me in spite of all the challenges that life has thrown at us.

Thank you, to my children, for loving me unconditionally and even when I was tired and stressed from all the early mornings and late nights.

Thank you, to Mom and Dad, for raising me to be a Jesus warrior and modeling true love, patience, and commitment. Thank you for always being my biggest cheerleaders.

I want to thank Miguel's mom, Mary, and dad, Gino. I am exceedingly grateful for all the encouragement and support over the years. Thank you for allowing me the freedom to call anytime to ask for sanctuary and opening your hearts and home to me even when it was the most difficult.

My precious Melinda, your wisdom and counsel were invaluable for the completion of this project. Your selfless sacrifice of time ensured that I could give God the very best. Thank you for being my editor in chief and friend.

I am so grateful to Carolyn for always having my back, Peggy for being an awesome mentor and a precious friend, and Connie for being a faithful listener. The Lord so perfectly sustained me during my darkest times by the precious prayers of you three.

Thank you, Teresa, for patiently working this thing through with me. You are the biggest reason it is not still sitting on my computer and waiting to be finished.

Thank you, Jill, for being the catalyst by which this study came to be, Jessica for continuing to trust me with your heart, and Emily, Christy, Autumn, Bethany, Narah, Mandy, and Mitsue for all your encouragement throughout this project.

Most importantly, thank You, my King Jesus, for continuing to pursue my heart and never letting me wiggle out of Your hand. Thank You for being my healer and my refuge in every circumstance of every day. You are worthy to have all my life.

CONTENTS

INTRODUCTION

Weeping may last for the night, But a shout of joy comes in the morning. (Psalm 30:5)

Sweet daughter of the Most High God, I am humbled and blessed that you have decided to pick up this book. The fact that you are here, reading, and seeking healing means that you believe that God can fix the brokenness in your heart. I want to start by encouraging you, before you even begin, that healing *is* possible. The dead corpse of your marriage can be resurrected, and the shattered pieces of your heart can be made whole. Your marriage can be made even stronger and filled with more love and tenderness than it ever was before.

No matter what has brought you here today—

The need for healing in your wounded mind because of continual hateful thoughts or arguments

The repairing of your broken spirit after countless verbal attacks

The restoring of your courage after physical abuse

The rebuilding of your shattered heart after betrayal, infidelity, or neglect

—the God of the universe sees you and desires to close up those wounds and give you a fresh new vibrancy.

I recognize that you may be battling intense anger at this very moment. Whether it's anger at God or your spouse, it's okay. The Almighty, Creator of heaven, is big enough to handle your anger. I implore you to keep at Him. Don't give up on Him or this study. Keep going back. Keep beating on His chest, until He wraps His arms so tightly around you that your arms become tired from the pounding and you collapse in His hands.

Let the tears pour out until you feel the tender hand of your Maker stroking your hair and hear His gentle whisper in your ear. Listen as He sings over you and quiets you with His love (see Zephaniah 3:17). Let the Holy Spirit make you ever more aware that the renewing of your mind through the Word of God will set you free of heartache, negative thoughts, unforgiveness, and the sorrow.

Follow the advice of Paul in Philippians 4:8 and think on things that are true, honorable, right, and pure. We must be on guard against our own deceptive hearts and the lies of the enemy. It is far too easy to let our thoughts and emotions run away with us. But the Word of God is our offensive weapon against false imaginations. Allowing our thoughts to run wild and unrestricted is not obedience to the high calling of Jesus. Rather, we should recognize and receive this truth:

> *The weapons of our warfare are not of the flesh but have divine power to destroy strongholds. We destroy arguments and every lofty opinion raised against the knowledge of God, and take every thought captive to obey Christ.* (2 Corinthians 10:4–5 ESV)

I am honored to be on this journey with you, although I know it will be challenging. I know it will likely be painful for both of us, but we are up to the challenge. By the grace of the Lord Jesus, you and I are up for the challenge.

Please remember that this study is called *Hills and Valleys* because healing is a process, and you will have good and difficult moments. There will be moments when you will feel like giving up. Regardless of whether it has been three days, three months, or three years, you are on a journey, and the healing doesn't come over night. Keep looking to Jesus, the author and perfecter of your faith (see Hebrews 12:2), keep asking, keep seeking, and keep knocking. The door of God's mercy will be opened to you (see Matthew 6:33).

Please take a few moments to read Psalm 34, which is located on the next page, before you begin this study. We will become very familiar with it by the end of our time together, but let's allow it wash over us even before we step forward.

PSALM 34

I will bless the Lord at all times;

His praise shall continually be in my mouth.

My soul will make its boast in the Lord;

The humble will hear it and rejoice.

O magnify the Lord with me,

And let us exalt His name together.

I sought the Lord, and He answered me,

And delivered me from all my fears.

They looked to Him and were radiant,

And their faces will never be ashamed.

This poor man cried, and the Lord heard him

And saved him out of all his troubles.

The angel of the Lord encamps around those who fear Him,

And rescues them.

O taste and see that the Lord is good;

How blessed is the man who takes refuge in Him!

O fear the Lord, you His saints;

For to those who fear Him there is no want.

The young lions do lack and suffer hunger;

But they who seek the Lord shall not be in want of any good thing.

Come, you children, listen to me;

I will teach you the fear of the Lord.

Who is the man who desires life

And loves length of days that he may see good?

Keep your tongue from evil

And your lips from speaking deceit.

Depart from evil and do good;

Seek peace and pursue it.

The eyes of the Lord are toward the righteous

And His ears are open to their cry.

The face of the Lord is against evildoers,

To cut off the memory of them from the earth.

The righteous cry, and the Lord hears

And delivers them out of all their troubles.

The Lord is near to the brokenhearted

And saves those who are crushed in spirit.

Many are the afflictions of the righteous,

But the Lord delivers him out of them all.

He keeps all his bones,

Not one of them is broken.

Evil shall slay the wicked,

And those who hate the righteous will be condemned.

The Lord redeems the soul of His servants,

And none of those who take refuge in Him will be condemned.

Week 1

BLESS THE LORD
PSALM 34:1–3

Welcome to the first week of study, dear one. Please take a few moments to pray and ask the Holy Spirit to open your heart and mind to the things that He desires to speak to you through this lesson. It may also be helpful to ask Him to show you any unconfessed sin in your heart or things that may be keeping you from hearing Him clearly.

As we begin this journey, my desire is for us to learn to look for the hand of the Almighty King in every circumstance. Though we go through times of suffering and pain, Jesus, our King, is ever present, ever purposeful, and always worthy of our attention and praise. Our healing will begin and end with giving glory to the Lord. It is in lifting Him up and finding opportunities to praise Him that our hearts will truly find peace and healing.

The heart of our King is ever attentive to us; therefore, let us be ever so attentive to Him. As Psalm 123:2 says, "Behold, as the eyes of servants look to the hand of their master, As the eyes of a maid to the hand of her mistress, So our eyes look to the Lord our God, Until He is gracious to us."

His graciousness is evident in our healing and transformation. We cannot heal ourselves. We cannot transform ourselves. Only the gracious power of the Holy Spirit is able to accomplish the things that must be accomplished in us. So we look to His hand.

Hopefully over the next few weeks, we will gain a fresh perspective on our circumstances and obtain the proper tools for handling our struggles. Firstly, I want us to see that pain and sorrow are not the enemies of our souls, but rather, they are blessings through which God moves, changes us, and brings our souls into deeper communion with Himself.

Oswald Chambers describes our trials in this way.

> My attitude as a saint to sorrow and difficulty is not to ask that they may be prevented, but to ask that I may preserve the self, God created me to be through every fire of sorrow … We say that there

ought to be no sorrow, but there is sorrow, and we have to receive ourselves in its fires. If we try and evade sorrow, refuse to lay our account with it, we are foolish. Sorrow is one of the biggest facts in life; it is no use saying sorrow ought not to be. Sin and sorrow and suffering are, and it is not for us to say that God has made a mistake in allowing them.

Sorrow burns up a great amount of shallowness, but it does not always make a man better. Suffering either gives me my self or it destroys my self. You cannot receive your self in success, you lose your head; you cannot receive your self in monotony, you grouse. The way to find yourself is in the fires of sorrow. Why it should be so is another matter, but that it is so is true in the Scriptures and in human experience. You always know the man who has been through the fires of sorrow and received himself, you are certain you can go to him in trouble and find that he has ample leisure for you. If a man has not been through the fires of sorrow, he is apt to be contemptuous, he has no time for you. If you receive yourself in the fires of sorrow, God will make you nourishment for other people.[1]

The reality of pain and sorrow are very present for you and me, and it is useless for us to fight against them. We ought to seek the purpose that God has called us to in the midst of them. They are for His glory, and He will bring us through them in order to make us blessings to others.

It may seem inconceivable right now that any blessing could come from what you've been through. Let me assure you now that our mighty King is fully capable of doing "immeasurably more than all we ask or imagine, according to his power that is at work within us" (Ephesians 3:20 NIV). My own life and marriage are a testament to that, as are those whom I have had the privilege of journeying with.

Father God,

I lift my sweet sister to You today. You know she is hurting so deeply and struggling to find peace. You know that she is angry—angry with her husband and You. Nothing in her heart is hidden from You. Help her know that Your chest is big and strong, and that she can beat on it because You can take it.

I pray that as she screams and pounds on You, You will wrap Your arms around her and hold her ever tighter. Let the strength of Your arms still her beating and the gentleness of Your voice quiet her heart. Melt away the anger and show her Your perfect love.

Teach her, God, that You are her refuge and the place of safety where she can hide. When she can't pray, let Your Spirit pray for her with groaning that is too deep for words. Teach her to rest in You. Help her to find hope and peace in Your love and in constant presence with her.

I ask all this for your glory. I pray this in Jesus's name.

Unless otherwise noted, questions can be most easily completed using the New American Standard Version of the Bible.

DAY 1: I WILL BLESS THE LORD AT ALL TIMES

My mouth will speak the praise of the Lord, And all flesh will bless His holy name forever and ever. (Psalm 145:21)

Thank you, dear friend, for inviting me to journey with you along this very difficult road to healing. I hope you have put on some sturdy hiking boots, grabbed a handful of tissues and a cup of tea, and packed your Bible and a pen, as we have some serious climbing to do this week. I am anxious and excited to begin traveling with you.

Hopefully, you have been able to read Psalm 34 already. If not, please take a minute to do that now. In verses 1–3, we see David crying out in praise to the Lord. David was committed to finding opportunities to praise his God regardless of the circumstances that surrounded him.

In verse 1, he says that the praise of the Lord will *always* be in his mouth. I don't know about you, but that can be an extremely difficult objective for me to accomplish most days. This is true particularly on the days when I have felt as though I were trudging through the valleys of death and darkness.

If anyone experienced the valley of death, it was David. As he penned this psalm, he had just run from King Saul, whom he had loved and served in the king's own house. While fleeing for his life, David pretended to be crazy and then found himself in hiding yet again (see 1 Samuel 21:10–15). In the midst of his despair, however, he said, "I will bless the Lord at all times." Instead of becoming angry with Saul, calling down curses upon him, or picking up arms against him, as we so often do when we've been attacked or wounded, David said that he would magnify the Lord at all times. He then challenged us to join him, saying, "And let us exalt His name together."

Notice that David also said, "The humble will hear it and rejoice." The humble, those who are willing to be taught of the Lord and recognize their need for Him, hear the praise on David's lips and rejoice. Wow! When we are walking through a trial and we manage to praise God in spite of the hardship, others see it and rejoice. We then become a shining image of the glory of the Lord and a cause for them to praise God.

The New International Version of the Bible translates verse two in this way, "I will glory in the Lord; let the afflicted hear and rejoice." We, the afflicted, hear others glorying in the Lord, and are compelled to rejoice with them. Likewise, they hear our praise, and begin rejoicing over what God has done for us.

Unfortunately, some of us have allowed fear, anger, anxiety, and bitterness to have a residence within our hearts for some time. Rather than allowing this to continue, let us learn to set our minds on what is good, pure, and true. Let us begin today to lay them down and take up joy and peace instead. Romans 12:2 says that we need to be transformed by the renewing of our minds. Let's look at how to practically accomplish this.

Read Philippians 4:4–9.

1. In verse 6, what are the three things Paul says you ought to do?

_____

_____

_____

_____

2. What does he say will happen if you apply these principles?

_____

_____

_____

3. Where does verse 5 say that the Lord is?

_____

_____

_____

_____

4. What does that mean for your circumstance?

_____

_____

_____

_____

5. List some of the things that cause bitterness or a lack of forgiveness to remain in your heart and that replay in your mind about yourself, your husband, your marriage, or your past relationships.

_____

_____

_____

_____

6. How does your heart respond to seeing those evil thoughts written on paper?

_____

_____

_____

_____

7. Explain what verse eight says you ought to do to replace your destructive, anxious thoughts.

_____

_____

_____

_____

Take a couple of moments right now and ask the Father to forgive you for believing those lies and to help you overcome them with the truth of Jesus.

8. What are some true, lovely, pure, admirable, excellent, and praiseworthy things about your husband and marriage that you can begin thinking on instead of the anxious thoughts?

_____

_____

_____

_____

In Philippians 4, we see Paul explaining the secret to having joy. In order to renew our minds, remove the old wounds, fill our hearts with healing, and begin restoring the love we once had in our marriages, we must choose to think on the things that are good and praiseworthy. It is also necessary to learn to praise God in the midst of our struggles. Paul said that we are to present our requests to God *with* thanksgiving. This means that *in spite* of all the heartaches and frustration, we need to be looking for opportunities to thank the Father for all that He has done for us.

Paul also says that we need to rejoice always. Sometimes, it seems near impossible to think that we would be able to rejoice in the midst of such deep sorrow and suffering, but our God is worthy of our praise, regardless of our circumstances. He has sent His Son to die for us, provided us with the Holy Spirit, granted us fellowship with Himself, and promised to never leave us no matter what circumstances we find ourselves in. If all that weren't enough, He has given us life eternal in heaven with Him. These are things worth rejoicing over, even as we walk through the valley of the shadow of death.

Let's look at some things that we can praise the Lord for and discover how great His love is for us. Please take some time to read Psalm 45 and let it soak in. Perhaps reading it two or three times or reading it aloud will help enable your mind to absorb the truths within it.

Notice in verse 1 that this psalm was written by the sons of Korah, who were chastised by God in Numbers 16 for speaking against Moses and Aaron in the wilderness. In spite of the sins of their fathers, younger generations of Korah are used by the Holy Spirit to prophesy about Jesus the Messiah and speak of

His Beloved. As you read, note all the ways we see these men acknowledging how the Messiah is worthy to receive our praise and adoration.

9. What stood out to you the most in this psalm?

_____

_____

_____

_____

10. According to this psalm, how is Jesus dressed? What does He smell like?

_____

_____

_____

_____

11. What else do the writers spend a lot of time talking about?

_____

_____

_____

_____

12. Read the following verses to discover who the Bible is referring to when using these titles: queen, princess, and daughter of the King.

2 Corinthians 11:2

The bride of Christ is _____.
                                                             (your name)

Isaiah 61:10

_____ is dressed with salvation as a bride dressed in jewels.
(your name)

Isaiah 62:5

God rejoices over_____ as a bridegroom rejoices over his
bride.   (your name)

The church, the people of God, (you and I) are called the bride of Christ. If we
are His bride, we are also His princesses, daughters of the King, and queens
of God.

13. What do the writers of Psalm 45 say about you, Jesus's princess? How are
you dressed? How does the King feel about you?

_____

_____

_____

_____

14. How does He handle His enemies (your enemies)?

_____

_____

_____

_____

15. What is your heart's response to these things?

_____

_____

_____

_____

16. Psalm 45 says the Mighty One has His arrows in the hearts of His enemies.
According to the following passages who are the enemies of the King?

James 4:4

_____

_____

_____

_____

1 Peter 5:8

_____

_____

_____

_____

Isaiah 63:10

_____

_____

_____

_____

1 John 3:8

_____

_____

_____

_____

Satan, his angels (demons), and those who are committed to the ways of this world are the enemies of God and His people. Satan is on the hunt for those whom he may devour. In John 10:10, Jesus tells us that Satan's purposes are to steal, kill, and destroy. He will stop at nothing to steal your joy, kill your peace, and destroy your marriage.

17. However, according to Romans 16:20, what will the God of peace soon do?

_____

_____

_____

_____

18. How does this relate to the King in Psalm 45?

_____

_____

_____

_____

19. How do these passages give you hope and the courage to step forward into the future?

_____

_____

_____

_____

Psalm 45 reminds us of the beauty, attractiveness, strength, majesty, and glory of our Warrior King. It speaks of His justice, humility, and the joy that surrounds Him. It encourages us that Jesus, our King, can and will crush the demonic presences that are battling hard against our marriages. Verse 4 says that Jesus rides out in victory and that He has made us victorious by His own blood. We are able to sing His praise and make the darkness flee because He has already won the war!

DAY 2: THE LORD IS ALMIGHTY

The voice of the Lord splits and flashes forth forked lightning. (Psalm 29:7 AMPC)

When we look at who God is, we can't help but praise Him regardless of our circumstances. My heart's desire is that you and I begin, end, and fill each day with thanksgiving and praise. If we can learn to worship our King in spite of our heartbreak, the healing will come much more quickly—and more effortlessly. I have also found that victory in spiritual warfare is much more achievable, if not entirely dependent upon, our worship and thanksgiving.

Be assured, my friend, that this battle for our marriages, is an intensely *spiritual war*. As we learned yesterday, all the power of hell is set on destroying the sons and daughters of the Most High. What better way to achieve that than to remove us from the most valuable relationships we have on this earth. We are in the fight of our lives, dear one.

However, we also learned yesterday that victory is already ours. Revelation 12:11 says that the saints (that's you and I) will triumph over Satan "because of the blood of the Lamb and because of the word of their testimony." Jesus is the Victor who has won the war by His blood. We have the power to overcome the enemy by the words of our praise. It is truly amazing how the enemy flees and the clouds begin to dissipate as we cry out to the Lord in praise.

Jesus is the Great Judge who will bring justice for us. He is our Rescuer and our Beloved. Let us learn to rejoice in Him and give Him all the praise that is due His name, so that we can shine with the light of His glory.

Read Psalm 29 and then pray through the words as the Spirit of God reveals Himself to you.

1. How does your heart respond to what is spoken about the power of God in this psalm?

_____

_____

_____

_____

2. List the seven things that the voice of the Lord is or does.

_____

_____

_____

_____

Let's pick apart this psalm and see if we can dig a little deeper. Let's look beyond what we can see on the surface. Start by reading verse 1 in the version below and note the use of the word *ascribe* with regard to God's glory and strength. Then look up this word in the dictionary.

> *Ascribe to the Lord, O sons of the mighty, Ascribe to the Lord glory and strength.* (Psalm 29:1)

3. According to the dictionary definition of *ascribe*, what are we to do?

_____

_____

_____

_____

In addition to attributing or accrediting honor *due* to the Lord, David insists that we "worship the Lord in the beauty of holiness" (Psalm 29:2 NKJV).

4. Have you ever thought of the Lord's holiness as being beautiful?

_____

_____

_____

_____

5. What do you consider beautiful? List a few of your favorite things of beauty.

_____

_____

_____

_____

When I think of beauty, my first thoughts run to Niagara Falls. The sheer mass of them and the volume of water rushing over those rocks every day are enough to make one stand in complete *awe*.

Though I've never seen the Falls in person, scrolling through pictures on the Internet brings me to tears. It is incredible how majestic, massive, and commanding they are, yet they are so beautiful. The water is an intense blue, but as it falls off the sides of the rocks at impressive speeds, it turns a snow-white color and remains that way until it crashes into the river below. There it returns to quiet crystal-blue. I can only imagine how magnificent the falls are in person. But what is it about holiness that's beautiful?

6. Read the following verses and write what holiness *looks* like.

> *And you shall make holy garments for Aaron your brother, for glory and for beauty. So you shall speak to all who are gifted artisans, whom I have filled with the spirit of wisdom, that they may make Aaron's garments, to consecrate him, that he may minister to Me as priest.* **(Exodus 28:2–3 NKJV)**

The _____ garments worn by Aaron were to be for _____ and _____.

These garments were for the purpose of _____.

> *Our holy and beautiful temple, Where our fathers praised You, Is burned up with fire; And all our pleasant things are laid waste.* (Isaiah 64:11 NKJV)

The temple of praise, the place where God dwells, is _____ and _____.

> *Look down from heaven and see, from your holy and beautiful habitation.* (Isaiah 63:15 ESV)

Heaven, God's place of habitation is both _____ and _____.

The holy garments of Aaron and the priests had to be the most intricate, beautiful pieces of clothing known to humankind at that time. They were adorned with jewels and gold, and were made with the finest cloth and the most artistic needlework. The comparison for us today would be the priests wearing Armani tuxedos. If they were women, they would wear Vera Wang wedding dresses. God required His priests to be beautifully adorned because He is beautiful. They were to be a reflection of Himself: the ultimate High Priest.

Likewise, God's holy temple was to be stunning. Imagine the Sistine Chapel or the Great Wall of China, which are works of absolute wonder and majesty. They boast of elegance of craftsmanship and incomprehensible engineering. The Almighty King is a God of order and purpose. He is beautiful and holy. Everything that bears His name must also display the beauty of His intelligence, wisdom, and holiness.

7. Read 1 Corinthians 6:19–20 in your own Bible and write down the place where God's temple is now located.

_____

_____

_____

_____

Paul says that you and I are now the temple of the Holy Spirit. We are glorious and beautiful because His holy presence dwells within us. We reflect all the majesty of His splendor and holiness. We sparkle as the Niagara River, full of color and brilliance. We roar with the same power and magnificence as the Great Falls when we sing the praises of the King.

Let's return to Psalm 29 and take a look at verse 7 again. The New King James version says, "The voice of the Lord divides the flames of fire. The New International Version says, "The voice of the Lord strikes with flashes of lightning." Imagine with me for a moment what that would be like. The King opens His mouth to command that our enemies be conquered. As His voice begins to sound, lightning flashes out in forks of power.

Reflect on the intense force of electricity contained within a single bolt of lightning. It is capable of destroying homes, burning down forests, and stopping the beat of a human heart. As the lightening words of God strike our enemies, their hearts stop and their flesh is burned. When His voice flashes against the barriers that stand in front of us, they are suddenly turned to dust and ash. The places where sorrow and bitterness have been dwelling are reduced to rubble.

The very same power that strikes like lightening to destroy our enemies also resides within us because the Holy Spirit dwells in us. His power is available to change our hearts, minds, and attitudes, as well as our husbands' hearts.

8. How does it encourage you to know that this power is available to you every day?

_____

_____

_____

_____

9. In Job 37:5–7, what are the things that God does?

_____

_____

_____

_____

According to David Guzik, the phrase, "He seals the hand of every man, That all men may know His work," in verse 7 refers to the weather's power to cause people to stop their work.[2]

10. Keeping this in mind, what do you think God expects us to do when we can't go outside because He has sent heavy rain or snow?

_____

_____

_____

_____

When we are unable to do our usual work, it is God's expectation that we take that free time to reflect on Him. He seals up our hands so that we may stop and learn to truly know *His* work.

Sometimes rain comes in the form of water on the ground. Right now, as we sit here, rain seems to be coming in the form of tears on our cheeks. The Creator of the heavens and the Almighty sender of rain wants us to use this season of clouds and darkness to look to Him and "know His work." Oh, that we would truly see and *know* the faithful, tender works of the Lord for us! Let's pray that we would begin to look at our storm as an opportunity to see the hand of God working in our lives and in the lives of those around us.

11. Take a moment to praise God for His power in your life and over your circumstances. Then read and pray the prayer below with me.

_____

_____

_____

_____

Father,

You are the Almighty Creator of the universe. The sun and stars are at Your beck and call. You know them each by name, and they exist to bring You glory. Yet Your tender hand is upon every detail and circumstance in each of our hearts. You have not forgotten or left us out in the rain that causes us to feel as if we are drowning. Rather, You have allowed the darkness of the world to move around us for Your own hidden purposes, which we may never know on this side of eternity. We humbly ask that You open our eyes to see Your hand move and Your power work. Teach us, Holy Spirit, to know Your work and to praise God for it. We ask in the name of Jesus so that His name may be lifted up in our hearts and in our lives. Amen.

Let's return once more to Job. As the man whom the Creator bragged about to Satan, Job endured much suffering and trial. In the midst of losing all his cattle and children, Job never cried out against God, but he did cry out in complaint of the intense grief that had beset him. He was in agony and wondering what he had done to deserve such trials.

The Lord spoke to him out of the *whirlwind*, which is also translated *storm*, saying, "Who darkens counsel by words without knowledge?" (Job 38:2 NKJV). In other words, who was he to speak against the acts of the Almighty? The Lord goes on to say, "Prepare yourself like a man; I will question you" (Job 38:3 NKJV).

Let's look at what the Almighty asks Job. Read Job 38:4–21.

The grilling of Job's knowledge continues for two more chapters and ends with, "Shall the one who contends with the Almighty correct Him? He who rebukes God, let him answer it" (Job 40:2 NKJV). After reading (or as Job experienced it, hearing) all that the Almighty has done and all that He knows, we fall on our face in awe! We repent of our complaints and rejoice over the magnitude of His greatness.

Look again at verse 19 and reflect on where the "dwelling of light" resides. We now know where the sun goes at night, but at the time, Job didn't. This made more sense to him because of his lack of knowledge. He would have understood that the Almighty King of creation was the commander of the sun, causing it to set every night and calling it out again each morning.

The magnificent sun, with all its fire and fury, does not scorch our planet, burn up our plants, or dry up our rivers because the Almighty has set it in the exact place that it needs to be in order to provide light and energy without destroying the earth. He "takes it to its territory" and knows "the path to its home" (the place where it goes at night).

Pretend for a moment that you don't know where the sun goes at night. Imagine the King of the universe asking you, "Do *you* know where I put the sun when it disappears from the earth each day? Do you know how it gets there or by what power it comes up again?"

12. How does that make you feel? In what ways does it cause you to praise the Almighty?

_____

_____

_____

_____

13. Ponder our modern knowledge of the sun and explain how the vast power and workings of the solar system move you to even greater awe than Job could have fathomed.

_____

_____

_____

_____

After watching the science fiction movie *Sunshine*, I gained a new appreciation for the power of the sun. It is fascinating to learn how intensely powerful the sun is and that it has its own gravity and weather. The sun was so incredibly beautiful that when the people in the movie looked at it for extended lengths of time, they became mesmerized. It became a form of worship for them. They couldn't get enough of sitting before its glory. They would sit in the observation room for hours, staring into the majesty of this heavenly being. How much more should we sit in awe of the King of creation, knowing that He is the One who has mapped the path for the sun's going down and coming up again? How much more should we worship His majesty?

Worship Him with me today. Praise Him for the victory you have in Jesus and the greatness of His majesty. He is supremely worthy of all our adoration!

DAY 3: THE LORD IS FAITHFUL

Therefore know that the Lord your God, He is God, the faithful God who keeps covenant and mercy for a thousand generations with those who love Him and keep His commandments. (Deuteronomy 7:9 NKJV)

Let's take a moment to remember what we learned yesterday about the greatness of the Almighty and begin this study with a word of praise.

Father, our King,

We praise You this day for Your ever-present goodness to us. We praise You that You are the Lord who sits as King over all the earth and its workings. You were King during the flood, and You are Ruler still. You rule over our lives and over our circumstances. You are so worthy of praise, for at Your voice, the forests are stripped bare, and the wilderness is shaken. Please cause us to continue to see with our hearts the glory of Your majesty. Teach us to worship You in the midst of our trials. In Jesus's great name, we ask. Amen.

Let's look at the faithfulness of our God, beginning in Exodus 34:1–7.

1. What do you notice about God in this passage?

_____

_____

_____

_____

In the New International Version's translation of verse 6, the Lord speaks of Himself, saying, "The Lord, the Lord, the compassionate and gracious God, slow to anger, abounding in love and faithfulness."

2. God calls Himself faithful. What does that mean to you?

_____

_____

_____

_____

3. According to verse 6, *"God is the* _____ *and* _____
God, _____ *to anger,* _____ *in love*
and _____*."*

Many translations use the word *truth* rather than *faithful* in this verse. The Hebrew word is *'emeth,* which means firmness, faithfulness, truth, sureness, reliability, stability, or continuance.[3] *'Emeth* stands as the foundation of all that can be known as absolute.

In other words, the love, compassion, and provision of God's unmerited favor (His grace) are as reliable as the ground you walk on—or more so when you consider that the earth is bound to shake and tremble from time to time. God's favor and compassion will not move or shift beneath your feet. The ground is sure to be beneath you. You will not wake up one morning and find that you no longer have a place to stand when you rise from your bed. So too, you will not wake up to find that today is the day, your Rock and Refuge has decided not to show up for your rescue. He will not be absent in your trial. He will not decide to pass judgment on your circumstance rather than show mercy on your heartache.

Let's consider the notorious woman at the well as an example for the Lord's faithful goodness. In John 4, after confessing to have had multiple husbands and a current adulterous relationship, we see that she had laid herself bare before Jesus. She had prostituted her heart and body to multiple men and denied the law that she knew was God's truth. She was empty, lonely, and rejected by society. Read her conversation with Jesus in John 4:7–27 and notice what Jesus did not say to her.

4. What could Jesus have rightfully said to this sinful woman?

_____

_____

_____

_____

For the sake of ease, let's call this woman Rachel. As she spoke with Jesus, Rachel anticipated judgment and hostility. She had been mistreated all her life, shamed, and ridiculed for her bloodline, lifestyle, and place of worship, but Jesus was neither judgmental nor hostile toward her. Rather, He said to her, "The hour is coming, and now is, when the true worshipers will worship the Father in spirit and truth; for the Father is seeking such to worship Him." Jesus shattered every stereotype and prejudice she had ever known by inviting Rachel to join with the "true worshipers." He neither blamed her nor accused her but instead, offered her peace and healing.

Hebrews 13:8 says, "Jesus Christ is the same yesterday and today and forever." If the same Jesus who spoke to Rachel at the well dealt with her in gentleness and love even while she was deep in sin and doubt, what does that mean He will do for you and me?

5. What does Jesus say to you in the midst of your unpleasant circumstance?

_____

_____

_____

_____

The faithful God of peace will neither blame us for our failings as wives, mothers, friends, or daughters, nor accuse us of being the cause of our husbands' choices. He will not respond to our anger with wrath or rebuke us harshly for wrestling with thoughts of divorce.

> My beloved spoke, and said to me:
>
> "Rise up, my love, my fair one,
>
> And come away."
>
> (Song of Songs 2:10)

He may reveal places in our hearts that are lacking. God may show us things that we need to surrender to Him, so that peace can come into our hearts and make us more like Himself. He may show us things we have done that have placed a wedge between ourselves and our husbands, friends, or others. Then He will call us on to higher and greater things. He will not condemn us.

6. Look again at verse 14 and note what Jesus says of the water that He gives in contrast to the water from the well.

_____

_____

_____

_____

The water Jesus offers us is refreshing and fulfilling. He says we will never thirst again when we come to drink from Him. We will not thirst for security in our spouses or the fulfillment of our deep longings to be drawn from our marriage. We will not expect our fears to be quieted by our husbands.

Jesus is the water that quenches all those desires. Yet we must be faithful to come to Him and draw from Him. We must be willing to lay all those things at His feet. We must trust that He is the faithful giver of the water that refreshes and restores us.

Hebrews 11:6 says, "Without faith it is impossible to please Him, for he who comes to God must believe that He is and that He is a rewarder of those who seek Him." Ironically, we cannot produce within ourselves that kind of God-pleasing faith.

Paul says in Ephesians, "For by grace you have been saved through faith; and that [faith is] not of yourselves, it is the gift of God" (Ephesians 2:8). We must come to the well (Jesus) and ask Him to grant us the "gift of God" (the faith) to be saved from ourselves, our fears, our doubts, and our hurts.

7. Read John 4:13–14 one more time. Jesus says, *"Everyone who drinks of this water will _____; but whoever drinks of the water that I will give [her] shall _____ again."* Write that word once more. You and I will "_____ *thirst*" again.

So faithful is the King to give us the water of His life, blood, Word, and comfort, which He says with all *'emeth* (truth, sureness, reliability, and continuance), will provide for us to *never* thirst again. The faithfulness of God reigns from the farthest corner of the universe to the deepest hidden recess of your heart. It is equally huge and insurmountable, and minute and indistinguishable. His faithfulness cannot be overcome or thwarted. It cannot be overwhelmed or left helpless.

He is the God who will not be stopped. He is "The Rock! His work is perfect, For all His ways are just; A God of faithfulness and without injustice, Righteous and upright is He" (Deuteronomy 32:4).

Jesus is as sure as the ground beneath our feet. He does not move, and because He is faithful, we too are immovable.

8. According to Psalm 16:7–8, what makes you and I immovable?

_____

_____

_____

_____

Read Hebrews 10:22–23 in below.

> *Let us draw near to God with a sincere heart and with the full assurance that faith brings, having our hearts sprinkled to cleanse us from a guilty conscience and having our bodies washed with pure water. Let us hold unswervingly to the hope we profess, for he who promised is faithful.* (**NIV**)

9. What do these two verses speak to you with regard to the things we've learned today?

_____

_____

_____

_____

10. How does Hebrews 10:22–23 apply to your current circumstance?

_____

_____

_____

_____

11. What can you believe about your King after reading these passages today?

_____

_____

_____

_____

Even as we walk through the valley of the shadow of death and our broken hearts ache so deeply that our physical bodies convulse in pain, our King is faithful. Even when we fall to the floor and weep in sorrow or scream in anger, our King is faithful. Even when the path to recovery seems distant, dark, and dangerous, our King is faithful. He is ever present in every circumstance, in every fear, in every regret, in every victory. He is present in every step.

Take a few moments now to praise the King for His faithfulness. Praise Him that you can come to Him and praise Him for the promises that you can believe He will accomplish.

> *For no matter how many promises God has made, they are "Yes" in Christ. And so through him the "Amen" [the "so-be-it" or "truth"]⁴ is spoken by us to the glory of God.* (2 Corinthians 1:20 NIV)

Praise Jesus that His written Word is available to you every day, for the purpose of your strengthening, your encouragement, the building up of your faith, and the tearing down of strongholds. Praise Him that He is *the same, yesterday, today, and forever.* Amen!

DAY 4: THE LORD IS SOVEREIGN

Oh, the depth of the riches both of the wisdom and knowledge of God! How unsearchable are His judgments and unfathomable His ways! "For who has known the mind of the Lord, or who became His counselor?" (Romans 11:33–34)

We will never know the joy of self-sacrifice until we surrender in every detail of our lives. Yet self-surrender is the most difficult thing for us to do. We make it conditional by saying, "I'll surrender if …!" Or we approach it by saying, "I suppose I have to devote my life to God." We will never find the joy of self-sacrifice in either of these ways … Our Lord is our example of a life of self-sacrifice, and He perfectly exemplified "I delight to do Your will, O my God …" He endured tremendous personal sacrifice, yet with overflowing joy. Have I ever yielded myself in absolute submission to Jesus Christ?[5]

Jesus was able to sacrifice all of His own will and desires because He fully trusted in God's sovereignty. Although the path laid before Him was full of agony and sorrow, and though He knew one of His closest, most trusted friends would betray Him, He walked the road of human affliction with joy. He did not cry out in anger for the suffering of His soul, as I, and possibly you, have done. He did not question the Father's goodness, or ask, "Why have you allowed this to happen?" as you and I so often do. Jesus, knew and trusted God's purposes. He therefore, willingly yielded Himself "in absolute submission," as Chambers says, to God's established plan for His life. What an incredible example!

Take a moment to pray and ask the Spirit of God to speak to your heart today. Then read Matthew 27:27–46.

Never Once

by Matt Redman, Jason Ingram, and Tim Wanstall

Standing on this mountain top

Looking just how far we've come

Knowing that for every step

You were with us

Kneeling on this battleground

Seeing just how much You've done

Knowing every victory

Was Your power in us

1. Note all of the ways Jesus's body was broken.

_____

_____

_____

_____

2. Read verses 45–46 again. Describe what you think it must have felt like to be abandoned by God.

_____

_____

_____

_____

I have never been abandoned by anyone and certainly not by my father. I can only imagine the pain and sorrow that comes with that kind of loss. However, the rejection that I experienced was excruciating enough to know that when a person is forsaken, it will leave a scar on his or her soul forever.

The feeling of abandonment that Jesus must have endured is unfathomable. His God, the lover of His soul and the One with whom He had perfect intimacy, turned away from the crucified Jesus. The grief had to have been unbearable. How could we even imagine the agony of His cry, "My God, My God, why have You forsaken Me?" (Matthew 27:46). Yet Jesus knew there was a purpose. He willingly said, "Not my will, but yours be done" (Luke 22:42).

3. According to 1 Peter 2:23, why did Jesus endure such agony?

_____

_____

_____

_____

If Jesus could willingly receive the beatings and rejection because He entrusted Himself to the One "who judges righteously" and knew that all would be made right in the end, how much more ought we to be able to trust Him? Yet for some of us, Jesus's trust in God doesn't easily translate to our own. If you're like me, you need more motivation and a little more proof that He can be trusted.

Let's seek out the King's trustworthiness to handle our every heartache. As you read the following passages, take time to meditate on the sovereign (*absolute power and control over all things*) hand of the King in *every* circumstance of your life and in the lives of *every* person who walks this earth.

4. Read the following verses in your own Bible and then fill in the blanks.

1 Chronicles 29:10-13

"Both riches and honor come from You, and You _____ over _____, and in Your hand is power and might."

Psalm 103:19

"The LORD has established His throne in the heavens, And His _____ rules over _____."

Isaiah 66:1–2

"Heaven is My _____ and the earth is My _____ … For My hand made _____, Thus all these things came into being … But to this one I will look, To [the one] who is _____ and _____ of spirit, and who trembles at My word."

John 3:35

"The Father loves the Son and has given _____ things into His hand."

Acts 17:24-27

"The God who made the world and all things in it … is Lord of _____ and _____ … He Himself gives to all people _____ and _____ and _____ things; and He made from one man

every nation of mankind to live on all the face of the earth, having determined their _____ times and the boundaries of their habitation."

1 Timothy 6:15–16

"Which He will bring about at the proper time—He who is the blessed and only _____, the _____ of kings and Lord of lords, who _____ possesses immortality and dwells in _____ light, whom no man has seen or can see. To Him be honor and eternal dominion! Amen."

Hebrews 1:3

"And He is the radiance of His glory and the exact representation of His nature, and _____ all things by the word of His power."

Colossians 1:16–17

"For by Him _____ things were created in heaven and on earth, [things] visible and invisible, whether thrones or dominions or rulers or authorities; all things were created and exist _____ Him [that is, by His activity] and for Him. And He Himself existed and is before all things, and in Him all things _____ together. [His is the controlling, cohesive force of the universe]." (AMP)

In 1 Timothy 6:15, the word *sovereign* is the Greek word *dynastēs*, which is translated in the King James Version to mean "'potentate,' a monarch or ruler."[7] *Dynastēs* also means, "a courtier, high officer, royal minister, someone of great authority."[8]

Paul is telling Timothy that Jesus is the supreme ruler of all things, or as David Guzik says, "The One who alone has all power and strength, who rules over the universe from an *occupied* throne in heaven."[9]

The Holy Spirit wants us to understand it the same way. The throne, the place of authority, power, and judgment of our King, has not been left unoccupied or haphazardly left to be attended by a prince, a dignitary, an imposter, or some other careless or apathetic personage. No, the absolute rule and attention to every detail of His Kingdom are in the careful, tender hand of the One who created it and died to redeem it.

The sovereign God of the universe upholds the world and every person in it. That means you and me. Every tear that falls from our eyes, every thought of regret, and every question "Why?" are seen and heard by the One who occupies the throne. He alone is able to correct all the wrongs that have been done to us, as well as the wrongs we have done to others.

5. Considering the meaning of sovereignty, what is your heart's response to the character and power of God presented in the above scriptures?

_____

_____

_____

_____

Let's return now to Jesus and look a little closer at what occurred before He was arrested and sentenced to die. Read the account of His arrest in the Garden of Gethsemane and carefully watch who is in control of each event.

6. In Matthew 26:51–56, Jesus said all that was about to happen was to be done in order to fulfill the _____.

7. Luke 22:53 says that Jesus was with the temple leaders "day after day" and that they were unable to lay a hand on Him. Now it was the hour of _____.

8. The same thing is spoken in John 18:1–9. Jesus tells the Roman troops who have come after Him, "I am _____."

John's is the only gospel to record the event in which the soldiers and officers of the Roman guard fell back. I love this account so much because in it, we see who is really in control during the arrest of Jesus. Matthew records Jesus reminding Peter that He has twelve legions of angels at His beck and call, and that if He desired it, God would send them instantly to His aid. Of course, the power and might of one angel would have been sufficient, but Jesus wanted us to know that in terms of spiritual warfare, He commands all the troops of heaven (which is probably far greater in number than twelve legions).

Yet, Jesus didn't need *any* angels to fight this thing. He is God, remember? This is what makes John's account so exciting. A troop of Roman soldiers and temple officers numbering in the hundreds showed up to arrest Jesus at night. That way, the things they were doing illegally would not be seen by the people or suspected by Jesus. It was to be a surprise attack. They must have realized that Jesus had the power to withstand them, for they felt it necessary to bring a large company of soldiers.

Jesus did not intend to resist them, but His name and His power were so great, they couldn't help but draw back and fall to the ground when He spoke to them that He *is* the *I am*. Just imagine a couple hundred of Rome's finest trained warriors and mercenaries, who were hardened and fierce, showing up to arrest just one man. Then He makes them all fall at His feet by the mere speaking of His name.

Even in the midst of His arrest, Jesus wanted everyone to know, He was *still* in control. Because He went willingly to the cross, He was not overpowered, overwhelmed, or tricked. He knew exactly what He was doing. As He told the disciples, it was done this way so that the scriptures might be fulfilled. He ordained all the events of that day and maintained their order perfectly, so that everything that was spoken in scriptures would come to pass.

So too, the King of creation orders all that enters our lives, both good and bad. He is the Almighty ruler of all things, and He "upholds the universe by the word of his power" (Hebrews 1:3 ESV). Thus, we are able to trust that everything He allows into our lives has a purpose. We can be confident that He will cause "all things to work together for good to those who love God, to those who are called according to His purpose" (Romans 8:28).

When we follow the example of Jesus by fully submitting ourselves to the plans of God and yielding our own will, we can then be "confident of this, that he who began a good work in you will carry it on to completion until the day of Christ Jesus" (Philippians 1:6 NIV). In spite of all the fear, regret, sorrow, and unanswered questions that linger before us, we are able to rejoice because of the glory that will come from the things He has already done and those that are yet to be accomplished. We can stand in awe of God's goodness and power and worship Him for His mighty hand on our lives.

9. How will you view God differently after reading of His sovereignty?

_____

_____

_____

_____

10. In what ways might you view your circumstance differently?

_____

_____

_____

_____

11. Knowing that God has been absolutely in control through all you've endured, what are some of the questions you would still like to be answered?

_____

_____

_____

_____

12. After having read today's passages, how will you be able to trust your King more in the midst of your trial?

_____

_____

_____

_____

Jesus trusted Himself to the sovereign Father because He knew the reward would be worth the journey. Although we still wrestle with the knowledge that God could have altered our circumstances and prevented us from walking this road, we can trust that He has a greater purpose than what we currently see.

Hold tight, dear one, to the King and His Word. Let His arms be your place of refuge and His power be the confidence you need to move forward today. Praise Jesus as you journey through your day, believing that He has the power to do "immeasurably more than all we ask or imagine" (Ephesians 3:20 NIV). He is your sustainer and your peace. He is with you on every mountaintop, and He will carry you through every valley, no matter how dark or dangerous it is.

DAY 5: GOD IS GOOD

I would have despaired unless I had believed that I would see the goodness of the Lord In the land of the living. (Psalm 27:13)

I have a feeling this is going to be an emotional, challenging day for us both. It is difficult to look into our heartbreak, know that our sovereign God had the power to prevent it, and not be angry with Him. It's even more challenging to believe that He is good in spite of the things that have happened in our lives.

My desire for us today is to learn to love and trust Him above all else, even when the world around us seems to be falling apart. If our hearts cannot feel safe with our heavenly husband, we will never be able to fully heal and feel safe with our earthly husband. So let's pray before we begin and ask God's Spirit to flood us with understanding and humility so that we can receive and believe His Word today.

Father,

Please open our hearts and our minds to know You more intimately today and cause us to receive, internalize, and take to heart all that You have planned for us. Help us to believe You with God-pleasing faith and to respond to You with deep adoration for all the goodness You have shown us. In Jesus's name, we ask. Amen

By now, you are probably becoming familiar with my appreciation for Oswald Chambers. His wisdom is both encouraging and challenging. I love what he has to say about the goodness of God in the midst of life's trials. Chambers says, "We must be merciful to God's reputation. It is easy for us to tarnish God's character because He never argues back; He never tries to defend or vindicate Himself."[10] In other words, it's very easy for us to make assumptions about or accusations against the sovereign King because He will not fight back. We begin to think within ourselves that we must be correct in our assertion because we have not been rebuked. This is a very dangerous road to travel.

When we begin to focus on the wounds that God has ordained for us rather than on the God who ordained them, we lose sight of His glory and purpose.

We begin to defame Him in our minds, and regrettably, our hurt turns to resentment. Resentment turns to bitterness, which then leads us to slander Him to others. This is a grievous sin. It is an error against our Maker. It brings me to tears, even to have to type it.

Before we can go any further in today's study, it may be necessary to stop for a moment and confess the way we have slandered the King in our hearts. If this has been true for you, please pray this passage in Psalm 51 with me.

> *Have mercy upon me, O God, According to Your lovingkindness; According to the multitude of Your tender mercies, Blot out my transgressions. Wash me thoroughly from my iniquity, And cleanse me from my sin. For I acknowledge my transgressions, And my sin is always before me. Against You, You only, have I sinned, And done this evil in Your sight—That You may be found just when You speak, And blameless when You judge.* (Psalm 51:1–4 NKJV)

The Father isn't obligated to explain Himself to us. He doesn't need to give us a reason to honor His desires, for as we learned yesterday, He is the Sovereign Ruler over all eternity. Just as any king waves his hand to give a command and all the subjects scramble to do it, our King has all authority and the right to expect the same of us. Although He doesn't force it upon us as an earthly king would. He is tender and gracious, permitting us to think and speak freely of His character and purposes.

However, we must be careful. There can be grave consequences in our hearts if we are not vigilant to keep ourselves disciplined to the truth of the Father's goodness. These consequences will manifest themselves in our own attitudes and lives. Then they will spill out and into the lives of others if they are left unchecked. We must be purposeful to continue to renew our minds by meditating on God's Word.

1. Please read and respond to Psalm 145:8–10.

Father, I thank you today because You are

_____

_____

_____

_____

2. In Psalm 68:7–20, do you see something new in God's character that you have not seen before or have forgotten about? What do you see?

_____

_____

_____

_____

3. What do verses 19–20 say about our King?

"[He] daily bears our _____, [He is] the God who is our _____. God is to us a God of _____; And to God the Lord belong _____ from death."

Most Bible translations say that to the Lord belongs "escape from death" or "deliverance from death," but I really love that the New American Standard Bible says, "To the Lord belong *escapes* from death" (emphasis mine). Isn't it interesting that the word *escapes* is plural? Doesn't it often feel as though the deathtraps in your valley are all around you like a minefield and just waiting for you to make one wrong move?

If you bring up your wound to your husband at the wrong time, "Boom!" If you see something that reminds you of your wound, "Boom!" If your children poke, prod, or speak insensitively to you, "Boom!" All the death and destruction that follows causes regret. There doesn't seem to be a way of escape as you try to navigate this treacherous valley, which is engulfed in dark, looming shadows.

Praise God. To Him *belongs* the escape from death. He is good, and He will faithfully guide you as you look to Him. He is the light in your darkness and the One who daily bears your burdens.

As we continue to look to Jesus's example of submitting ourselves to the authority of God, which we learned yesterday, let's consider again His attitude toward His death. Read Matthew 16:21–23.

> *From that time Jesus began to show His disciples that He must go to Jerusalem, and suffer many things from the elders and chief priests and scribes, and be killed, and be raised up on the third day. Peter took Him aside and began to rebuke Him, saying, "God forbid it, Lord! This shall never happen to You." But He turned and said to Peter, "Get behind Me, Satan! You are a stumbling block to Me; for you are not setting your mind on God's interests, but man's.*

Just prior to this conversation, Jesus had asked His disciples who they thought He was. Peter said, "You are the Christ, the Son of the living God." Jesus confirmed this to be true and then told them not to tell it to anyone else. From that time on, He began teaching them that He must die. He knew that if the people understood His identity, they would feel as Peter had and prevented His death.

The disciples were to keep the revelation of His identity a secret until after His death and resurrection. But Peter couldn't bear the thought of his Lord suffering at the hand of evil men. In essence, Peter was insisting that his understanding of the world was greater than Jesus's was. His view of the circumstance was that it would be cruel and unfair for Jesus to die, which in fact it was, but it was necessary—and *good*—nonetheless. Your circumstances and mine may also be unfair or even cruel, but even still, God and His purposes are good.

Jesus wouldn't let Peter step in and protect Him against the coming brutality because although Peter's intentions were good in his own eyes—defending his King as any good servant would—he did not understand the purposes of God. Jesus even called him a stumbling block. Imagine the shock and confusion Peter must have felt after Jesus rebuked him so sharply. Yet Jesus gives him the reason for the urgency of the reprimand. Peter's mind was not set on God's interests.

Often, our minds are set on our own agendas or the interests of our children or our spouses rather than on God's. This is especially challenging when we or someone we love are suffering, hurting, or in an unchanging, unfair situation. However, we can be confident as Jesus was because we know as He knew that our Father's plans are good.

4. In what ways have you been setting your mind on human interests rather than on those of God?

_____

_____

_____

_____

As you read the following verses, ask the Holy Spirit to reveal the goodness of the Father to you and to give you a scripture, which you may claim as a prayer and promise for your heart's healing. I have intentionally not placed any interpretation or fill-in-the-blank questions for these verses. This leaves them open for the Holy Spirit to speak directly and specifically into your personal circumstance.

5. Read and identify the Father's goodness toward you in the following passages.

Deuteronomy 6:18–19

_____

_____

_____

_____

Zephaniah 3:12–17

_____

_____

_____

_____

Nehemiah 1:7

_____

_____

_____

_____

Joel 2:26–27

_____

_____

_____

_____

Ecclesiastes 5:18–20

_____

_____

_____

_____

Joshua 1:5–9

_____

_____

_____

_____

Isaiah 43:1–4

_____

_____

_____

_____

Matthew 7:7–11

_____

_____

_____

_____

Jeremiah 29:10–14

_____

_____

_____

_____

Psalm 34:8

_____

_____

_____

_____

6. What passage struck you the most? Why?

_____

_____

_____

_____

7. How does this new revelation change your perspective on your circumstance?

_____

_____

_____

_____

8. How does it give you hope and peace for the future?

_____

_____

_____

_____

In my own struggle, I have wrestled with many questions regarding God's goodness balanced with His absolute sovereignty. I have cried out to my King, asking, *What promise can You give me that says I won't be hurt again? How can I be sure this will all work out? How do I believe Your promises in the midst of not knowing whether or not Your plan is for more sorrow and suffering?*

I don't know the answers to these questions, for myself or for you, but I do know that our King *is* good. I know that He has promised good for me and you. The best thing that I can say to both of us is that when we continue to ask, seek, and knock with faith and confidence, He hears, and He will answer. We must keep believing that God will say, "Yes," until He says, "No." If the *no* does come, then we accept it from His hand, believing that He has something *better* in store.

I am so grateful that for the past several years, my Redeemer has answered my heart's prayer with, *Yes! Yes, I will heal and restore your marriage. I will give you a new beginning and a more blessed life with your husband.* More importantly, however, He has given me a deeper and more intimate knowledge of Himself, His glory, and His goodness. For that, I am immensely thankful.

I know He desires to do the same thing in your life. He desires to heal your marriage and to give you a beautiful, joyful relationship with your husband. More importantly, He desires that your heart be truly His and that you be willing to fully trust and believe Him in all things. Your relationship with Jesus is the Holy Spirit's first and most important priority.

King Jesus is worthy of all our allegiance, honor, and praise because He is forever *good*. Believe Him today and worship Him. He came to this earth willingly to die for you and for me. He is good. Hallelujah!

As we complete this week, let us return to Psalm 34, remembering all that we have learned through the study. Our Father, the King, is the faithful, almighty, sovereign, gracious Creator of all things. He is *good*. He is worthy of our praise, adoration, complete surrender, and allegiance. He is our protector and the refuge that we can run to at any time. We can know by faith that He is present in all our circumstances and attentive to each detail of our trials.

Jesus knows the pain of rejection because He too bore the sorrows of betrayal. He is the one and only giver of peace. Those who see His peace and glory in us will also praise Him for the work that He has done in us, so let us bless the Lord.

I will bless the Lord at all times; His praise shall continually be in my mouth. My soul will make its boast in the Lord; The humble will hear it and rejoice. O magnify the Lord with me, And let us exalt His name together.
(Psalm 34:1–3)

Week 2

Seek the Lord
PSALM 34:4–8

As we begin this week's lesson, I am humbled yet again that you are walking this journey with me. It is an immense honor, and I don't take lightly the privilege and responsibility to walk alongside you in this healing process.

I have tears in my eyes and sorrow in my heart as I begin writing today. I have seen so much brokenness and pain in the eyes of the women who have walked this road before us. There is so much temptation to become bitter and hardened. The topics we are discussing are heavy, and our burden is wearisome, but Jesus is our strength. May He also be our source of courage as we step forward into deeper and more difficult issues. May He keep our hearts soft and heal our wounds rather than allowing us to become callus and cynical.

Hang in there with me, dear one. Keep your eyes on Jesus and remember that He can handle all your fears and doubts. Ask Him to show you how to practically live out the truths we are learning, as they apply to your individual circumstance. This journey is going to get harder for both of us, before it gets easier.

DAY 1: I SOUGHT THE LORD AND HE ANSWERED ME

I sought the Lord, and He answered me, And delivered me from all my fears. (Psalm 34:4)

When King Solomon had finished building the Temple of the Lord, he prayed that the Lord would hear the prayers that the people offered in the Temple.

> *If they take thought in the land where they are taken captive, and repent and make supplication to You in the land of their captivity, saying, "We have sinned, we have committed iniquity and have acted wickedly;" if they return to You with all their heart and with all their soul … and pray toward their land which You have given to their fathers and the city which You have chosen, and toward the house which I have built for Your name, then hear from heaven, from Your dwelling place, their prayer and supplications, and maintain their cause and forgive Your people who have sinned against You. (2 Chronicles 6:37–39)*

Solomon, knowing that he was a sinful man, living among sinful men, and foreseeing that his people would turn against God, cried out to the Lord and asked that God would hear them from heaven and forgive their sins. He asked that the Lord would return them from the captivity God promised to send them into if they disobeyed. He asked that the Lord would return them to the land that He had given them: the land of His "rest," as Psalm 95:11 calls it.

In some ways, our current situation feels as if we were living in a land of captivity, doesn't it? You and I may not have been at fault, nonetheless, the sin of our spouses may have dragged us off into a form of captivity. Be it fear, doubt, strife, or pain, we've been carried away from the place of God's peace and rest.

1. Read 2 Chronicles 7:12–16 and write the Lord's response to Solomon in your own words.

_____

_____

_____

_____

2. In Isaiah 56:7, God says that His Temple is a house of _____.

The Temple that Solomon built was made of stone and metal, but the temple where the Lord currently lives is your body. As we learned last week, the Bible says, "Or do you not know that your body is a temple of the Holy Spirit who is in you, whom you have from God" (1 Corinthians 6:19).

In 2 Chronicles 7:16, God said, "I have chosen and consecrated this house that My name may be there forever, and My eyes and My heart will be there perpetually." It means that your King has chosen, consecrated, and set apart for Himself a temple in you. The Spirit of the living God dwells within you, and His eyes and His *heart* are with you perpetually. Wow!

3. In 2 Chronicles 7:15, what does God say that He will do for and in you, His temple?

_____

_____

_____

_____

4. According to verse 14, what does God require in order to hear our prayers?

_____

_____

_____

_____

5. Read James 5:16. What must we do to be healed?

_____

_____

_____

_____

When we repent of (turn away from) our sins, turn to God, and seek His face, He says that His ears will be open to us. He will hear from heaven and forgive our sins: our failings, unbelief, angry outbursts, hypocrisy, and bitterness. He will then heal our land: the place where we live, our hearts, our minds, and our physical being.

6. What part of your land needs the most healing or transformation right now?

_____

_____

_____

_____

7. Do you believe God can heal it? Why or why not? Be honest. Your King can take it (He already knows anyway).

_____

_____

_____

_____

It is not difficult for me to believe that the *Creator* of the universe is *capable* of healing my wounds or fixing the messes I have made of my life. But I confess that I sometimes struggle to believe that He *would* choose to make things right or take away the pain.

The deep wound that came with the betrayal I had suffered left me feeling like I was standing before the throne of God with cupped hands, which held only the dust that had once been my heart. It had been broken before, but now it was beyond broken; it was crushed. As I sat in the dark hours of the morning crying out to God, I wondered, *How is it even possible to fix this? Will He really make it all right again? Can He?*

Maybe you're wrestling with these feelings too. Maybe you're wondering if you'll ever be able to forgive completely or if the anger or pain will stop pounding in your heart. Let me assure you, dear one, Jesus *can* heal it, and the pain *does* dissolve … but only in the presence of the perfect Healer. We must *continue* to take our grief to Him with open hands and lay our anger at his feet, again and again and again. We must trust that He will answer our pleas and turn the ashes—the dust of our hearts and possibly our marriages—into beauty (see Isaiah 61:3).

Read Matthew 7:7–11 in the Amplified Bible.

> *Ask and keep on asking and it will be given to you; seek and keep on seeking and you will find; knock and keep on knocking and the door will be opened to you. For everyone who keeps on asking receives, and he who keeps on seeking finds, and to him who keeps on knocking, it will be opened. Or what man is there among you who, if his son asks for bread, will [instead] give him a stone? Or if he asks for a fish, will [instead] give him a snake? If you then, evil (sinful by nature) as you are, know how to give good and advantageous gifts to your children, how much more will*

your Father who is in heaven [perfect as He is] give what is good and advantageous to those who keep on asking Him.

If we who are sinners and prone to selfishness are capable of giving good and loving gifts to our children, how much more is the *good* Father going to lavish His *perfect* gifts on us? Notice what we must do in order to receive the good gifts from the King. We must keep asking, seeking, and knocking. It's a continual thing. Until the door of heaven is flung wide open and the pieces of your heart are fully intact again, keep praying, crying out, and pounding on the chest of the Father.

Look carefully at Matthew 6:25–34.

8. What is Jesus effectively saying?

_____

_____

_____

_____

Although Jesus is speaking about clothes, food, and drink in this passage, He is admonishing us to guard our minds from constantly running through all the cares of the world.

Psalm 127:2 says, "It is vain for you to rise up early, To sit up late, To eat the bread of sorrows; For so He gives His beloved sleep" (NKJV). Our Beloved does not want us to lie in bed at night fretting over what he did, she said, the hurts they caused us, or what so-and-so will think of us. All that strife is the bread of sorrows, which is no longer ours to eat. I don't know about you, but I have wasted *many* nights lying awake and fretting over what has been and what will be. Oh, those long dark nights of wrestling within myself. It was pure torture and torment that I caused myself. I often planned revenge or thought through what I would say if this or that happened.

But Jesus said that He is the Bread of Life. We are encouraged to eat of Him. He says that His burden is light and that He will grant sleep to His beloved.

That's you and me! If we seek first the face of our King and desire the presence of His kingdom in our lives, He will answer our prayers, grant us sleep, and heal all our wounds.

For our last reading of the day, let's look at our theme passage. Read Psalm 34:4–8 and pay careful attention to how your King reacts to your broken heart.

9. Respond to your Beloved about all that He has taught you today.

At the Foot of the Cross

(Ashes to Beauty)"

At the foot of the cross

Where grace and suffering meet

You have shown me your love

Through the judgment you received

And you've won my heart

Now I can

Trade these ashes in for beauty

And wear forgiveness like a crown

Coming to kiss the feet of mercy

I lay every burden down at the foot of the cross

_____

_____

_____

_____

_____

_____

_____

DAY 2: THE KING'S HEART FOR YOUR MARRIAGE

The angel of the Lord encamps around those who fear Him, And rescues them. (Psalm 34:7)

The journey for today's study has been quite a battle for me. Today's topic is my third attempt at writing this lesson. The first two topics that I began writing were thrown out by the Holy Spirit. I've since felt compelled to take this day and dedicate it to studying God's heart for marriage.

As I was reading during my personal study time the other morning, I ended up in Malachi. I had no plans to read there, but as I continued to look into the mirror of God's Word, I was taken aback by just how tenderhearted God is toward us, our heartaches, and especially our marriages. Would you take a moment to lay down all your preconceived ideas of marriage and look with me at what the Creator has to say about *His* covenant?

Read Malachi 2:10–16, being careful not concern yourself with what is said of the husband in the passage. Let's not spend our attention on our spouses and their wrongs right now. Rather, let's commit our minds to the Father's heart and *His* response to our husbands and to us.

1. Why does the Lord no longer accept with favor the offerings given by the men of Israel (verse 14)?

_____

_____

_____

_____

2. Who is the primary witness of your wedding vows (verse 14)?

_____

_____

_____

_____

3. Verse 15 says that the Lord God has made both husband and wife one in flesh and in spirit. Why?

_____

_____

_____

_____

4. The husband is to "guard [his] heart; remain loyal to the wife of [his] youth" because God hates _____
(verse 15 NLT). He says that divorce covers the husband's garment with _____

I am amazed anew at the incredible glory God has hidden away in the covenant of marriage. I have heard it said many times, especially by the younger generations, "Marriage is just a piece of paper, so why bother going to all the trouble and expense of getting married?" But when we take a closer look at who instituted marriage and why He did it, it brings a fresh understanding of the great depth and complexity regarding the gift of togetherness our Creator has given us.

First of all, God instituted marriage as one of the first forms of friendship, partnership, and government on Earth. He gave man an *ezer*, which is the Hebrew word for *helper*. This word means far more than a woman who washes dishes or files papers.[12] The word *ezer* is more properly translated *lifesaver*, as John Eldridge says in his book *Wild at Heart*. His ministry website, Wild at Heart, quotes the book.

The phrase [*ezer kenegdo*] is only used elsewhere of God, when you need him to come through for you desperately ... Eve is a life-giver; she is Adam's ally. It is to both of them that the charter for adventure is given. It will take both of them to sustain life. And they will both need to fight together.[13]

Soldiers in the army use the term *battle buddy* or *battle* to express the same type of partnership as Eve's camaraderie with Adam. The physical safety and emotional well-being of a soldier is highly dependent upon the quality of his battle. He knows he can trust a true battle buddy for everything. He knows his battle has his back in a firefight, will love on his kids, protect his wife, and guard his honor.

A similar roll to that of an army battle would be the air force's term *wingman*. You remember *Top Gun*. You know what I'm talking about. The wingman is the guy who's guarding the lead plane's rear blind spot and protecting him at all costs.

You and I, dear sister, were given as battle buddies or lifesavers to our husbands. Their honor and glory in raising children, their careers, their emotional well-being, and their lives are highly dependent upon our care and support of them.

That's why in Malachi 2:14 God says that we are "[his] companion and [his] wife by covenant" (ESV). The Creator intended us to be their companions, their partners, and a united front with them against all enemies and intruders. Cue the tears. I am crying here. Are you? I know that this is hard to think about when our partnership has been betrayed, abused, and even crushed, but it is God's heart for us nonetheless.

His desire is that we value each other and our partnership with a special preciousness. We are not only partners and confidants, but we have become *one* flesh. The English Standard Version says in verse 15, "Did he not make them one, with a portion of the Spirit in their union?" (Malachi 2:15). His heart is tender toward our relationship because His Spirit and His very presence are intertwined in our union.

When we have been betrayed and our vows have been neglected, not only have our own hearts been wounded but the very Spirit of the Most High is also offended and hurts with us. That's why He says in verse 16, "For the man who does not love his wife but divorces her ... covers his garment with violence" (ESV).

Let's pause for a moment before we discuss the violence and look at this concept of the garment in Ruth 3:7–13.

5. What does Ruth ask Boaz to cover her with?

_____

_____

_____

_____

6. According to Ruth 2:12, under whose wings has Ruth taken refuge?

_____

_____

_____

_____

Interestingly, the same Hebrew word is used in both of these verses. The word *kanaph* means "wing, extremity, edge, winged, border, corner, overspreading, or corner of a skirt or garment."[14] In chapter 2, Boaz first acknowledges that Ruth has taken refuge in the shelter of God's covering. Then she requests to take shelter under Boaz's wings.

Think for a moment of a mother eagle. Have you ever seen a documentary or a nature film that shows an eagle in her nest with her young? Her massive wings spread out over all the chicks and shelter them from cold, wind, and rain, up high on the cliffs. The small helpless birds, which are without feathers, are not blown out of the nest or frozen by the fierce winds because their mother covers them. She protects them from the danger of falling out and crashing onto the sharp mountain rocks. She hides them from predators. Her soft wings are their comfort. They fear nothing and lack nothing when she is present.

So it is with God's covering over us. His heart is tender toward us as a mother bird is tender toward her babies. Jesus said in Matthew, "How often I wanted to gather your children together, the way a hen gathers her chicks under her wings" (Matthew 23:37). He has called our husbands to also be tender toward and cover us.

The covering of a woman by her husband is so important to God. The oneness He has created between a husband and wife is so significant that

He even says that if a man lies with his father's wife, he has uncovered his father's own nakedness (see Deuteronomy 22:30). The father's honor and the son's future and prosperity are both put in jeopardy if the wife has borne her nakedness inappropriately. Deuteronomy says, "Cursed be anyone who lies with his father's wife, because he has uncovered his father's nakedness" (Deuteronomy 27:20). The same word (*kanaph*) that means *wings* or *covering* in the book of Ruth is also used here for *nakedness* or as some translations say it *skirt*. Because he is supposed to be the covering over his wife, when she has been naked before others, the man himself is shamed. It is as though he himself has walked around naked for all to see.

The symbolism of wings or covering was even brought into the wedding ceremony as part of Hebrew tradition. According to David Guzik, "Part of the marriage ceremony in Bible times involved the husband covering his wife with his garment as a symbol of the protection he brought her."[15] Rather than seeing the woman as only his housekeeper or his personal chef, the husband recognized his responsibility to display the image of God's own covering over His bride.

Marriage on earth is designed to represent our relationship to Jesus. Revelation calls the Church, "the bride of Christ," and in several references in the Old Testament, God is called the people of Israel's husband. Most explicitly, our King says of us in Ezekiel 16:8,

> *When I passed by you again and saw you, behold, you were at the age for love, and I spread the corner of my garment over you and covered your nakedness; I made my vow to you and entered into a covenant with you ... and you became mine.* (ESV)

He has covered us with his *kanaph* and made us His bride.

This concept of God's marriage to us gives an added significance to the marriages of people on earth. The loving groom Jesus, who gave Himself up for His bride, expects earthly husbands to do the same so that His tender love toward His own bride would be manifested to the watching world. As Ephesians says, "Husbands, love your wives, just as Christ also loved the church and gave Himself up for her" (Ephesians 5:25).

God hates divorce because it defames His own relationship with His beloved people (see Malachi 2:11, 16). The representation of Jesus's love for His church is marred, and the watching world develops a distaste for the things of God because His image becomes corrupted in its eyes.

Yet as Guzik says,

God's heart is *always* for repentance, forgiveness, and reconciliation in marriage. We have sinned against God far worse than any spouse could sin against us, and God does not divorce us—though He has every right to."[16]

Our marriages were designed to demonstrate the same kind of mercy and forgiveness that God has given us. Although we sin against our spouses and they against us, we are called to forgive each other and to reconcile. "There is no doubt that God hates divorce because it destroys what He loves—marriage is the LORD's holy institution which He loves."[17]

His heart is broken, and He is personally offended when our marriages are offended, betrayed, or devalued or we are wounded. We are covered by Jesus's garment, and our marriage is meant to display His glory. When we are exposed or shamed, so is He (see Isaiah 53:3–6, Hebrews 12:2, and Deuteronomy 27:20).

Now that you have a better understanding of the covering, return to Malachi 2:16. We are told that a man who divorces his wife covers his own garment with violence. When translated, the Hebrew word *chamac* means "violence, damage, false, injustice, oppressor, unrighteous, or unjust gain."[18]

7. What do you think it means when God says that divorce covers the garment with violence?

_____

_____

_____

_____

There are several thoughts on the interpretation of this particular verse. Some commentators have said that rather than saying the garment is covered with violence, verse 16 should read more like Psalm 73:6, which says, "The garment of violence covers them" (NASB). This would indicate that the violence is the divorce, and the covering, which they use as their justification, is the permission to divorce (given by Moses in Deuteronomy 24:1), according to the *A. R. Fausset Commentary.*[19]

Another interpretation is that the violence is done to the wife by *putting her away*. William MacDonald quotes Baldwin as saying the phrase is "a figurative expression for all kinds of gross injustice which, like the blood of a murdered victim, leave their mark for all to see."[20] This explanation makes the most sense to me because as we saw earlier, the word *chamac* means more than just violence. It is injustice, cruelty, and a cause of damage.[21]

Some Bible translations have actually employed this phraseology when interpreting the following passage. The New Living Translation says, "'For I hate divorce!' says the LORD, the God of Israel. 'To divorce your wife is to overwhelm her with cruelty'" (NLT).

The New International Version goes so far as to equate divorce with hate, "The man who hates and divorces his wife … does violence to the one he should protect" (NIV). I personally like this one because it takes us back to the covering—the symbol of protection. The man who removes his covering from his wife opens her up to all kinds of harm. She is made vulnerable to harm from the world in the form of criticism or judgment. She is vulnerable to other men by opening her up to enticement, temptation, or even harassment. Most tragically, she is left unprotected from the enemy, for Satan desires nothing better than to torment her. God sees this as a gross form of cruelty.

Divorce, neglect, and abuse of a spouse or of our vows are very serious offenses to God. He is tender toward us and toward our wounds. As Zechariah 2:8 says, "He who touches you, touches the apple of His eye." You are as precious to Him as His very sight. If you are harmed, He is also!

My goal in this discussion is not to cause guilt or additional hurt with regard to your thoughts on divorce. I want to make it clear that it is not wrong to contemplate divorce. You certainly have every right, according to scripture, to do so. I am not preaching on how you ought to move forward from here. My earnest prayer is that both you and your husband are pursuing reconciliation because you are holding this book. However, I am well aware that some wounds won't heal and some offenses are not recovered.

Some offenders refuse to change, and some hearts refuse to repent. That is not to say that the wounds, hurts, or offenses *can't* be healed, changed, or recovered because our great God *is* fully capable of miracles, but some people simply refuse to allow His hand to move them. My only goal is to open your eyes to how deeply the Father cares for your marriage.

I cannot speak to your specific situation, but Jesus can. Please take a few moments in prayer to seek the heart of your tender Husband, Jesus. Ask Him what parts of today's message are meant to move you. Ask Him to show you which direction He desires you to go and to give you the courage and strength to start on or continue along that path.

8. How has the Spirit of God ministered through today's study to your own circumstance?

_____

_____

_____

_____

9. What principles from today's lesson may Jesus be calling you to act on?

_____

_____

_____

_____

DAY 3: MARRIAGE ACCORDING TO SCRIPTURE

They looked to Him and were radiant, And their faces
will never be ashamed. (Psalm 34:5)

As we continue to seek the Lord and lay ourselves before Him so that He might hear our prayers, it is important to learn to view things as God views them. If we are to truly pursue Him, then we must seek to understand what His will and purposes for our lives are.

The Bible has much to say on the topic of marriage. Relationships in general are of great importance to our King—because He is relational. As we learned yesterday, marriage is of special interest to God because how we handle our marriage relationship, displays what God thinks of marriage and of us to our children and the world. We must be careful to honor God's reputation with our marriages and our perspective of them.

Today we are going to touch on just a few topics that affect our relationships on a daily basis. By no means will this be an exhaustive study, but I highly recommend that you dig deeper into God's Word regarding all of these topics and ask the Holy Spirit to reveal His truth to you in a fresh way.

Let's begin by praying. I really desire to hear God's truth for my life during this study. I pray that you do too.

Father,

We are so desperate for You. We need Your wisdom and supernatural revelation for our marriages now. Please open our hearts to Your truth and open Your Word to us in a fresh way. Please reveal Your truth as it is and not as we think it should or want it to be. Let Your Word shine light into our lives and bring change and healing to our hearts. It's for Your glory, Lord, and our good that we ask these things, in Jesus's name.

Do you know that you have an enemy and that it's not your husband or the other woman? It's not your children, parents, boss, or your neighbor. Do you know that your present circumstance and the heartache you've been suffering didn't come because your husband woke up one morning and said, "Today is the day I'm going to crush my wife and destroy my life"?

Read 1 Peter 5:6–10. Let's see if we can discover what's really going on with the painful, mean, ugliness of this life.

1. According to 1 Peter 5:8, *"Your adversary, _____ prowls around like a roaring lion, seeking [a marriage] to devour."*

2. But we must *"_____ him, firm in [our] faith, knowing that the _____ experiences of suffering are being accomplished by your [sisters] who are in the world"* (1 Peter 5:9).

3. Fill in the first blank with your name then finish the sentence based on what you just learned.

Similar suffering is being accomplished by our sisters throughout the world; therefore, _____ is _____ alone.

Because you and I have sisters everywhere "in the world"—but not of it—who are also suffering in similar circumstances, we are *not* alone. Our gracious King has given us sisters who have traveled this road before us, are right where we are now, and possibly will come up behind us. He uses these sisters to encourage and spur us on.

I'd like to take a few moments to pour some hope into your heart by sharing a couple of stories with you. My own heartbreak came when my husband was traveling with the army. He was pursued and tempted by another woman. We had been struggling to connect emotionally and physically, due to severe exhaustion. We were worn out from the spiritual battle, which we'd been fighting for months. In addition, we were awake all hours of the night with a challenging baby, and from my husband's demanding training schedule and his constant travel.

I knew he wasn't good and that we weren't good, but it was still a complete shock to me that he would fall so easily... Yet deep in my heart, I wasn't all that surprised (perhaps you too, experienced the same paradoxical feelings). I had been too hard on him, and I had not given him the grace that he needed while in the midst of a very trying time in his personal and professional life. Something had to give for him somewhere.

Nonetheless, it was, as you're well aware of, absolutely devastating. I had been a faithful wife, prayed for him, tried to encourage him, and done my best to drag some kind of affection out of him to meet my own needs, which I thought would help us reconnect. It took months to unpack how all the events that led up to the affair had played out like a perfectly arranged set of dominos. Once the first one tipped, they all followed brilliantly, as demonic forces breathed lies into my ears and his.

But God: In His incredible mercy, Jesus our Healer broke through all the hurt and baggage from years of mistreatment and bitterness and met us in our need. We fought an even more intense spiritual battle during the several months that followed. The enemy's presence in our home was tangible. We had to work at loving each other ten times harder than we had before. We had to lay down our pride and self-will in order to surrender to the Lord and to each other, in a way we had never known.

It was intensely painful and required every ounce of energy we had. But it was worth every minute. I am immensely grateful for all that the Lord has done and all the hard work and commitment of my husband to heal our relationship.

I have also had the great honor and privilege of walking alongside several dear friends as they have struggled to put their lives back together after their husbands' betrayals. One sweet friend wrote her story down, and in a precious act of vulnerability, she opened her heart to me and allowed me the privilege of reading about all that God had done for her. After a very painful affair, she and her husband were reconciled. They continue to work at a successful business partnership. She was the inspiration and Holy Spirit's prompting for me to write this Bible study. For that, I am eternally grateful.

Some of the ladies I've walked with have dealt with pornography (which *is* adultery, in case anyone is unsure) battles in their marriages. Others have discovered that their husbands have or have had emotional or chemical imbalances. Another woman watched as her husband packed up his belongs and left—forever. Some have battled emotional infidelity or emotional abuse while others have suffered from being blamed for their husbands' indiscretions.

Tragically, some of these marriages have been lost, but others have not. Many of these ladies are still married, happier, and more in love with their husbands than they have ever been. Regardless of the outcome, most have seen the glory of the Lord shine in their lives and learned to praise Him in any circumstance. They have become more dependent upon Jesus and have come into deeper and more intimate relationships with Him, which is the greatest glory of all!

In every circumstance and around every corner, my dear friend, Jesus is with you. All around the world, our sisters are suffering alongside us. We are not alone. Our enemy the devil is running rampant and ravaging marriages in God's Church. He knows that if he can destroy our families, we will not be able to shine the light of God's mercy and forgiveness on the watching world. Satan knows that broken families will struggle to raise a godly generation, which God desires. We do *not* have to succumb to the lies, which originate in the pit of hell. We *have* victory in Jesus.

Look again at 1 Peter 5:10.

> *After you have suffered for a little while, the God of all grace, who called you to His eternal glory in Christ, will Himself perfect, confirm, strengthen and establish you.*

4. How long will we have to suffer?

_____

_____

_____

_____

5. To what has God called us?

_____

_____

_____

_____

6. After you have suffered only a little while (compared to eternity!), the King, *"will Himself,* _____, _____, _____ *and* _____ *you."*

At this point, we are all groaning inside, aren't we? We wonder, *Suffer? Must we suffer? For how long?* The question I'm most frequently asked is, "How long did it take before you weren't hurting or angry all the time?" I remember asking the same thing of the two women who had walked the road of recovery before me. We always want to know when it's going to end.

Our loving King knows that we are hurting, and He groans with us. Remember, we are the apple of His eye. We hurt; He hurts. But this doesn't mean that He will end the agony prematurely. He has purposed to use it for our good. He intends to see us perfected in our commitment to Him, strengthened in our faith, confirmed in His will, and established in our love for His Son. The suffering has a purpose, dear one.

We must be willing to look past the pain and see the hand of the Father working in the sorrows, but He does not expect us to do it alone. Let's look at a few verses that discuss how we can traverse the murky waters to achieve victory.

Read 2 Corinthians 12:7–10.

7. Whose power is made perfect in us when we surrender our weakness and seek to walk in God's will?

_____

_____

_____

_____

8. Did Jesus remove the thorn from Paul's side? _____

What does this mean for your current thorn?

_____

_____

_____

_____

9. What does Paul say enables him and you to endure the suffering?

_____

_____

_____

_____

Paul said that the power of Jesus rested on him in the midst of His weakness. So rather than balking at God, crying, beating his chest, whining, screaming, or pouting, he simply relinquished himself to the purposes of the King and prayed for strength. More than that, he boasted in his own weakness and struggles because he knew that was the place of ultimate power. When we have surrendered in our minds to the place where we are completely helpless in and of ourselves, that's when the power of the Almighty is made perfect in us. This is incredible!

Let's look at one more passage before we move on. Please read 1 Corinthians 1:7–9.

> *Therefore you do not lack any spiritual gift as you eagerly wait for our Lord Jesus Christ to be revealed. He will also keep you firm to the end, so that you will be blameless on the day of our Lord Jesus Christ. God is faithful, who has called you into fellowship with his Son, Jesus Christ our Lord* (NIV).

10. Who keeps you firm to the end as you wait for Jesus to be revealed in your circumstance?

_____

_____

_____

_____

11. Verse 9 says that He will do this because *"God is* _____ *, who has called you into* _____ *with his Son, Jesus Christ our Lord."*

Though our strength and ability come from Jesus, we must also exercise wisdom. Solomon said in Proverbs 9:10, "The fear of the Lord is the beginning of wisdom, And the knowledge of the Holy One is understanding."

So as we seek the Lord and desire to know His purpose for us, He will begin to empower us with His wisdom. We need to pray for His wisdom to rest on us and for Him to teach us His understanding with regard to our marriages. It is important to receive all that He has spoken regarding our husbands and our marriages. We must begin to pray for the wisdom to know how to apply the principles of Scripture to our individual relationships in a practical way.

We all understand the concept of authority. We have teachers, pastors, managers at work, and governmental officials who are set in place over us. However, many of us (myself included) have rejected the authority of our husbands, the way an unbroken stallion kicks and bucks against its trainer.

I know this is a very challenging topic to address up front, so I will be brief here and come back to this later. But may I encourage you to lay down your hurt and anger for just a moment with me, and let's try to see things through the eyes of scripture. You may need to stop, pray, and ask the Holy Spirit to give you the grace, ability, and courage to set aside the things that hinder you.

Read 1 Corinthians 11:3, 7–12 and Ephesians 5:22–29

12. According to these verses, who is the head (authority) over you? Who is the head over him?

_____

_____

_____

_____

Let's not be distracted by all the hair cutting mentioned in these passages. That was mainly a cultural thing, but if you're concerned with it, I highly encourage you to research it in a commentary (blueletterbible.com is a great resource). The main point Paul is driving home here is that of authority.

The woman is the glory of the man, meaning she is a reflection of him just as he is a reflection of Jesus. If a marriage partnership is working correctly, the husband should be treating his wife with the highest honor and tenderness, as we see in Ephesians 5, so that she may see the love of her Savior through him. Likewise, she ought to be honoring and respecting her husband, just as she would her heavenly Husband. This displays the love of Jesus to the world and to their children.

We are not here to address what our husbands ought to be doing, but how *we* can be seeking to live out the wisdom of scripture. However, let's take a moment to understand what authority is *not*.

Take a look at 1 Peter 5:1–5.

13. According to verses 2–3, persons in authority are not to (circle all that apply)

> a. Lord it over those under their care
>
> b. Seek a position of authority for the purpose of dishonest gain
>
> c. Be an example to those under their authority
>
> d. Be angry, bitter, and harsh with God's sheep

Peter says that our husbands are not to lord their authority over us. They are not to abuse their authority for selfish gain. Rather, they are to shepherd us tenderly and with gentleness—our hearts, minds, and bodies—and to be an example to us with an eagerness to serve.

Dear friend, if your husband continues to mistreat, neglect, or abuse you, whether it's mentally, emotionally, or physically, I plead with you to seek godly counsel and get help. I would never counsel you to stay in an unhealthy environment. If you need to leave, please do so. With much prayer and counsel from others who love you and your husband and care for your marriage, take some time of separation to seek God's purpose for you.

My encouragement to women in these kinds of circumstances is always to spend some time away to seek Jesus and *His* will, with the full expectation of returning to the marriage in order to restore it. It is important to let your husband know why you are taking this time away. In a loving and respectful way, you need to express to him what has caused you to make this decision and give him the parameters for which you will return. He needs to understand that you love him, that you intend to be reunited with him, and the amount of time you expect to be away. I cannot express enough that this *must* be done in *love* with the utmost *respect* for your husband and the gravity of the separation. The purpose must be to pray and not to be spiteful or manipulative.

The Holy Spirit can change even the hardest of men, and even the most broken marriages can be restored. But we must use wisdom and approach all our decisions with prayer rather than self-gratification or self-preservation.

We have covered a lot of ground today. My head is spinning and my heart if very full. Is yours? Let's end today by meditating on one last passage. I'm not going to ask any questions with this one. I pray that you will linger here and ask Jesus what He desires for you to take away from it. Then you can respond to Him on the lines below.

> *To sum up, all of you be harmonious, sympathetic, brotherly, kindhearted, and humble in spirit; not returning evil for evil or insult for insult, but giving a blessing instead; for you were called for the very purpose that you might inherit a blessing. For, "The one who desires life, to love and see good days, Must keep his tongue from evil and his lips from speaking deceit. He must turn away from evil and do good; He must seek peace and pursue it. For the eyes of the Lord are toward the righteous, And His ears attend to their prayer, But the face of the Lord is against those who do evil." (1 Peter 3:8–12)*

Father, thank you that

_____

_____

_____

_____

Please forgive me for

_____

_____

_____

_____

Holy Spirit, by the power that raised Jesus from the dead and now dwells in me, please help me to

_____

_____

_____

My King, by that same power that is at work in me, please work in my husband to

_____

_____

_____

Thank You, Jesus,

That you are the Emmanuel, God with us. Thank You that Your Holy Spirit dwells within us and that in our weakness, Your power is made perfect. We love You, Lord. May we walk in a way that is pleasing to You today, and may the light of Your glory shine through us. Amen.

DAY 4: WOMEN ACCORDING TO SCRIPTURE

Submit yourselves for the Lord's sake to every human institution, whether to a king as the one in authority, or to governors ... and the praise of those who do right. For such is the will of God that by doing right you may silence the ignorance of foolish men. (1 Peter 2:13–15)

Congratulations, you have made it half way through week two. I know this has already been such a challenging study, and we still have much to dig into. My deepest prayer is that you are continuing to seek out the desires of your King and keeping your heart open to His purposes for you.

As we continue to venture down the dark, untamed, and sometimes frightening places of our healing, I want us to be sure that we are continually surrendering to the heart of Jesus. He so desperately loves us and deeply cares for our heartaches—even those we've caused ourselves. He sees our wounds. He has orchestrated our circumstances. His desire is to bring us out of the valley and onto the mountaintop of His glory.

Today as we consider what it is to be a woman of God (a married woman of God), I am mindful of the ups and downs that we will continually face in this healing process. Sometimes we feel great, and it seems like we can conquer anything that comes our way. At other times, it feels as though each step that we take is like walking through concrete. We wonder if we will ever get beyond the grief, feel normal again, or spend a day without thinking of the wound.

Sometimes we think, *What am I doing? I am such a fool to let this man walk all over me like this. He has betrayed my trust, broken my heart, and treated me so carelessly, why should I stay and continue to deal with all this? Doesn't he know I deserve better?* It feels so foolish to continue to return our hearts to the men who have betrayed us, doesn't it? It is so contrary to what the world tells us we should do. It says that we are strong, independent, and purposeful women. We don't need men, and we certainly don't need men who have treated us so harshly. It makes no sense to open ourselves back up to hurt and betrayal again.

Let's see what Jesus would say about these feelings. Read Luke 17:3–10.

1. It is the heart of our Savior that we (circle one):

---

a. keep score, reminding ourselves of our husbands' continual failings

b. tell the Lord *again* why we simply can't forgive this one

c. justify our irritation with a list of all the things *we* have *not* done to harm our marriages

d. forgive our husbands, knowing that we are not perfect, yet Jesus still continues to forgive us.

Jesus said that if our husbands offend us we are to forgive them. It is not foolish but wise to lay the sorrow and anger at the feet of Jesus, asking Him to be the judge between ourselves and our husbands. Though the world may tell us, "You're just being a doormat if you let him get away with this," we know the world is against us and God (see 1 John 2:15–17). Thus, we can't trust anything it says. Instead, let us lay down our rights and seek peace.

Before we go any further, I want to express my heart's deep burden for those who have been suffering beyond what the Lord requires of us. Dear sister, if your husband is harming you physically, is abusing you mentally or emotionally, or is manipulative and controlling, again, I plead with you to *seek help*. This lesson is not speaking to those who are suffering continually under an abusive husband or to those who have dealt with multiple episodes of infidelity. If your husband will not remain faithful, this is not true repentance. I don't presume to know what you should do or how you ought to proceed in your individual circumstance, but it is *imperative* that you find a godly woman, counselor, or pastor to give you wise counsel.

That said, I plead with the women who are seeking to be reunited to their *repentant* husbands to lay down those feelings of foolishness and pursue mercy and forgiveness. Sometimes peace and reconciliation come at a great price. Most often, the price is our own pride and self-will. Sometimes, however, it is financial, such as making sacrifices to pay off the hidden credit cards or changing health clubs or phone numbers. The cost may be inconvenient, as in the case of a woman I read about, who rid her home of Internet in order to help her husband refrain from pornography.

Let's review Jesus's thoughts on the cost of following God's purposes. Read Matthew 16:21–23 and respond to the questions.

2. Why did Jesus rebuke Peter?

_____

_____

_____

_____

Remember, Peter felt it was unfair for the Messiah, King of the world, to suffer and die. He believed that Jesus had come to overthrow the Roman oppressors. But Jesus had come to overthrow the real oppressors: sin and death. Jesus did not have the luxury of feeling sorry for Himself in all that He would endure, or of allowing His disciples to pity Him.

It is likewise necessary for us to believe that for the glory of God and the redemption of our marriages, we too must not pity ourselves. Rather, we take our example from the One who suffered most. We pray just as Jesus did, submitting ourselves to the will of the Father.

Not My will, but Yours be done. (Luke 22:42)

Let's look at some of God's purposes for us as wives while we count the cost of honoring the Lord in our marriages. Please return to 1 Peter 5:1–11 and answer the following questions.

3. According to verse 5, we are to clothe ourselves with _____ because *"God is opposed to the _____ but gives grace to the _____."*

4. Verse 7 says to cast all your anxiety upon Jesus. List the anxieties about remaining in your marriage that you are currently carrying.

_____

_____

_____

_____

5. How can you cast those cares onto the One who cares for you?

_____

_____

_____

_____

6. What do you think humbling yourself looks like within your marriage?

_____

_____

_____

_____

7. What is that going to cost you?

_____

_____

_____

_____

If I may, let me press in a little more, although I know it's getting hot in here. Please read and respond to Titus 2:3–5, 9, keeping in mind that whether you are young, old, a servant, or a master, these admonitions apply to all of us.

8. What attributes of a godly woman stood out to you the most?

_____

_____

_____

_____

9. Which attributes do you struggle most with displaying?

_____

_____

_____

10. Verse 5 says that we as women are to love our husbands and children, be kind, and *submissive*. Why?

_____

_____

_____

_____

Did you catch that? Paul says that women who do not love, honor, and submit to their husbands shame the gospel of God. Whoa! That is a tough one to swallow. Many of us find the concept of submission repulsive, especially after what we've been through, right? But we need to remember what we learned earlier of Jesus's heart for us to forgive our husbands. It is wise—not foolish—to seek to honor the Lord's commands. So in spite of feeling foolish and it being contrary to the world's perspective or advice, let's begin honoring the Lord in this area called submission.

Yesterday, we talked briefly about what submission is *not*, but let me give you a little more clarity. Submission is *not* dishonoring the Lord or being obedient to your husband if he asks you to sin. It is *not* enduring your husband lording his authority over you or being oppressive to you as a person (You ought to feel free to be yourself and express your personality). It is *not* being a doormat or never having an opinion or a say in family decisions.

Rather, it is humble surrender to the authority of your earthly king. This displays your absolute trust in your heavenly King to work out all the consequences of the decisions that are made. In order to really dig into what the Bible means by submission, return with me to Ephesians 5:22–24 in the Amplified Bible.

> *Wives, be subject to your own husbands, as [a service] to the Lord. For the husband is head of the wife, as Christ is head of the church, Himself being the Savior of the body. But as the church is subject to Christ, so also wives should be subject to their husbands in everything [respecting both their position as protector and their responsibility to God as head of the house].*

11. What things are we to be subject to?

a. Only those decisions with which we agree

b. Everything

c. Nothing

12. Why is this important?

_____

_____

_____

_____

We are to submit to our husbands as the God-given authority in our lives in *everything*, just as the church is to submit to Jesus in *everything*. Husbands are likewise to submit to God because they are held accountable to Him in *all* their decisions. This is a huge benefit for us. This is where you and I can take a breath and say to ourselves, *Regardless of how this thing turns out, I know that the Lord will take him to account on it.* That takes a lot of pressure and responsibility off our shoulders, my friend. This should be a relief to us, not a burden.

Submission is God's provision of protection for us. It is our *kanaph* covering—a blessing to us. We never have to fret over whether we have made the right decision. I don't know about you, but I've fretted many nights over whether a choice that I had made was the wrong one. When we simply honor Him in this command, what a relief it is to know that we can surrender these things to our husbands and trust that God will work out all the details for our good and His glory.

13. Which issues or concerns do you have the most trouble surrendering to your husband?

_____

_____

_____

_____

14. Right now, take a moment to surrender those things to your heavenly King first and then ask Him to help you submit to your husband in them also.

_____

_____

_____

_____

We're almost done. I know we've gotten our boots dirty today. Just hang in there with me a little bit longer. Take a deep breath, refill your teacup, and open up your Bible to 1 Peter 3:1–7. As you read, notice how many statements are addressed to husbands and how many are aimed at us wives.

15. Why do you think there are more commands spoken to women?

_____

_____

_____

_____

16. What spoke to you the most as you read everything that is addressed to us wives?

_____

_____

_____

_____

17. How does Peter say we are to win our husbands over to the Lord (whether they are unbelievers or disobedient Christians)?

_____

_____

_____

_____

What does "without a word" mean? Well, I'm quite sure it doesn't mean that we ought to nag about reading their Bibles, praying with us, or into going to church with us. I'm confident that it does not mean we should judge or criticize their every move or decision (small or great). I think it probably doesn't include making them feel like home is the least encouraging place to be.

On the contrary, I read somewhere a long time ago, and it has stuck with me, that we ought to be our husbands' biggest fans. It ought to be our goal to make our presence and our homes places where our husbands find refuge from a harsh world. They ought to be able to fall "heavy into [our] arms," in the midst of a world filled with "days of dust," as the *Mumford and Sons'* song "I Will Wait" puts it.

We can be contentious wives who are an incessant dripping like Proverbs 19:13 says, or we can be a ray of light and a cool, refreshing breeze to them in a world that beats down their self-esteem and tears at their manhood. May we be the women who speak, "Pleasant words [which] are a honeycomb, Sweet to the soul and healing to the bones" (Proverbs 16:24). And may we learn to pray rather than open our mouths when it comes to things that are not ours to speak.

Okay, back to our passage in 1 Peter.

18. What kind of spirit is precious to God (verse 4)?

_____

_____

_____

_____

Note that the text says *spirit* and not *voice*. Don't think that if you are a loud personality like me, you will be disqualified from this blessing. We loud types can still cultivate quiet gentleness within our spirits.

19. What does that mean to you? What might a gentle, quiet spirit look like for you?

_____

_____

_____

_____

Peter gives us a little peek into Sarah's secret to peace. She didn't let fear rule her decisions. She could have easily been consumed with the what-ifs of obeying her husband or the things that it would cost her to follow him all over creation. She was not shaken by the fear of what it would mean for her to leave her family and everything she had ever known. She did not fear financial ruin, the perpetual moving from place to place, loneliness, or even being taken advantage of by her husband. Sarah followed Abraham, "calling him master," and trusted God with all the implications of what that meant for her future.

20. What consequences do you fear will happen if you submit to your husband?

_____

_____

_____

_____

In 1 John 4:18, we read, "There is no fear in love; but perfect love casts out fear." The love of our Heavenly Father is absolutely perfect, and He is fully capable of handling all the fears that we hold in our hands today. If we love Him and believe in His love for us, all our fears are expelled. All that remains is quiet-hearted obedience. Let's ask Jesus to carry all our anxieties, casting our cares upon Him, and let us trust to Him the consequences of our husbands' decisions.

DAY 5: PRAYER ACCORDING TO SCRIPTURE

Delight yourself in the Lord; And He will give you the desires of your heart. Commit your way to the Lord, Trust also in Him, and He will do it. (Psalm 37:4–5)

I am so blessed and grateful that you had the courage to open this book back up again today. I know that at this point, you are probably thinking, *Wait, I thought this study was supposed to be about healing. I didn't sign up for another message about all the things I should do in my marriage.*

It may be hard to see it right now, but I promise that all these things are beneficial to our healing. As much as we may be the innocent victims of the wounding from our husbands, we are not innocent people. I think we can agree that you and I are both flawed sinners, failing to live up to God's standards. I think we can also agree that we have not always been entirely perfect in our behavior toward our husbands and that there is still room for improvement.

As we seek to improve our own behavior, another thing is true. Our respect for and willingness to submit to our husbands breathes life into them. In order to help them heal and move beyond their own failings, they need to know that we still believe in them. Unless your husband is a cold heartless man, I promise you, he is carrying around a huge amount of guilt and shame for his actions. If he has been unfaithful, he may also be dealing with the pain of separation from the other woman.

Again, I know this is a bitter reality to accept. You may be thinking, *He deserves to be in pain, and he doesn't deserve me to be considerate of his troubles. He needs to be taking care of me.* All of this may be true, but remember what we learned last week about entrusting ourselves to the one who judges righteously. Jesus will be the mediator. He will correct all the wrongs that have been done to us.

We are to be compassionate and merciful. So as you consider what your husband may be struggling with, remember that the Lord said that when two people give themselves to each other physically they become one flesh. It means that your husband joined himself to another person, and he was torn apart from her like two pieces of paper that have been glued together and then separated. Both are damaged. Like you, this man also has a mourning and healing process, which he has to work through. Your love, compassion, and respect toward him are necessary to help rebuild his wounded soul.

I know you probably want to scream at me and throw the book against the wall right now. That's okay. I would too. Go ahead. I'll wait.

Okay, now that you've got that out of your system, hear me out.

Your husband has been wounded somewhere along the way too. Whether it was the enemy completely deceiving him so that he fell into a trap, a wound inflicted by his parents, or a brutal blow to his ego at work, there is something under the surface that has caused him to turn against the Lord and harm you. Please understand, I am not excusing his behavior but only trying to help you understand that he must search out the Lord and find what has caused the failings in his own heart. He too must seek reconciliation with God and possibly the other person—whomever that may be.

My prayer is that you will begin to have empathy and compassion toward your husband and pray for him to be restored in his own personhood. If he is not whole and wholly surrendered to Jesus, your healing will be hindered as well. That's not to say that Jesus can't fully heal you apart from your husband, but it will be more challenging for you. The two of you are one flesh, remember? Your very being is intertwined with his, and both of you need each other to work this thing out—together.

Because this is such a tender, difficult task for us and we have been so terribly wounded, prayer is absolutely necessary. We cannot take on this task alone. We need our King to fight for us. So today, we will look at how to pray most effectively for our husbands and our marriages.

Take a moment right now and ask the Holy Spirit to open your heart so that you can receive all that He desires to teach you. Then let's dive in. In order for our prayers to be effective, they must first and foremost be done in faith. Let's consider a couple of examples. Please read Matthew 8:5–13.

1. In your own words, recount what happened in this passage.

_____

_____

_____

_____

2. Note what Jesus told the man in verse 13. *"It shall be done for you as you have _____."*

3. If Jesus said the same thing to you, "As you have *believed,* so shall it be done," what would be done for you with regard to your marriage?

_____

_____

_____

_____

4. What would that change about the way you currently believe and pray?

_____

_____

_____

_____

Now look at Matthew 9:18–26.

5. The synagogue leader said, *"My daughter has just _____; but come and lay Your hand on her, and she will _____."*

What? When someone has just died, is our prayer usually, "Lord put your hand on her and she *will* live"? The father, didn't say, "Maybe," "If you could," or even, "If it's your will." This man, with all boldness approached the Savior and said, "Come with me. Come be in my life and home so that my child may live."

When we feel that our hearts are like lifeless corpses or that our marriages are in the grave, do we pray, *Jesus, touch us so that we may live*? Do we have that kind of faith? Or do we get lost in the fretting and worrying about what will come of the future?

Oswald Chambers says, "It is not only wrong to worry, it is infidelity, because worrying means that we do not think that God can look after the practical details of our lives."[22] Not only are we living in unbelief when we pray without faith but it also appears that God is *offended* by it, just as you and I have been offended by the infidelity of our beloved. How can we ask God to do something in our lives when we turn around and think, *Well, He probably won't really do it*? How offensive that must be. Why even bother asking? Come with me to explore this concept a bit more.

6. What does James 1:5–8 say in regard to doubting and prayer?

_____

_____

_____

_____

7. According Hebrews 11:6, how do we please God?

_____

_____

_____

_____

I have a book of prayers (which I *highly* recommend getting your hands on if you can find it) called *Praying in the Word of God: Advancing Christ's Kingdom* by Kathleen G. Grant There is a section in the book on confessing the sins of the family. Kathleen uses this reference in Hebrews to pray, "Forgive us ... we have grieved you by not trusting your word and claiming your promises."[23]

Have you ever stopped to think that not claiming God's promises is something that we must be forgiven for? I certainly hadn't. Yet Hebrews says that we ought to be praying with complete faith. This word faith, or *pistis* in the Greek, means persuasion, assurance, or belief.[24] But if we want the Bible to be a commentary to itself, we can look in Hebrews where it explains to us what faith is. Look at Hebrews 11:1 in the different translations below. Try to let it sink into your heart.

Now faith is the assurance of things hoped for, the conviction of things not seen. (ESV)

Faith shows the reality of what we hope for; it is the evidence of things we cannot see. (NLT)

Now faith is the assurance (title deed, confirmation) of things hoped for (divinely guaranteed), and the evidence of things not seen [the conviction of their reality—faith comprehends as fact what cannot be experienced by the physical senses]. (AMP)

Did you get that? Faith is assurance, conviction, reality, evidence, and the title deed to the things that we don't see or haven't yet experienced or received. So in order to pray effectively, we must trust fully that God gives us the assurance that we have *already* received the things we have asked Him for.

8. But don't take my word for it. Let's let our King speak for Himself. Read and respond to the following verses.

John 14:11–14

_____

_____

_____

_____

Luke 11:9–10

_____

_____

_____

_____

Matthew 7:7–11

_____

_____

_____

_____

John 15:15–16

_____

_____

_____

_____

John 16:23–24

_____

_____

_____

_____

Lastly, John 16:26–27 in the Amplified Bible says,

> *In that day you will ask in My name, and I am not saying to you that I will ask the Father on your behalf [because it will be unnecessary]; for the Father Himself [tenderly] loves you, because you have loved Me and have believed that I came from the Father.*

I don't know about you, but that last one makes my heart leap in my chest. The Creator of the Milky Way and all the galaxies and the One who set the mountains in place and holds back the waves from overtaking the shore tenderly loves *me*. And *you*. Because of His great love, He hears our pleas. What joy!

9. How do these statements of Jesus increase your faith (confidence, assurance, conviction, and reality)? Respond in a prayer of thanksgiving to your King.

Now that we have a better grasp on faith in prayer, let's see what makes prayer effective. For reasons that I don't understand, it would seem that God wants us to recount His promises to Him. If we believe His Word, claim it in our circumstances, and pray it back to Him, there seems to be some mysterious movement in heaven. I am not trying to be mystical or give you a formula for guaranteed results by which you can manipulate God. I'm simply letting you in on a little secret about prayer.

Hebrews 4:12–13 says,

> *The word of God is living and active and sharper than any two-edged sword, and piercing as far as the division of soul and spirit, of both joints and marrow, and able to judge the thoughts and intentions of the heart. And there is no creature hidden from His sight, but all things are open and laid bare to the eyes of Him with whom we have to do.*

God's Word is alive. It is active. It moves us as we pray, and it moves the heart of the Father. He loves to fulfill His promises to us, but if we don't know them, how do we recognize them when they've been fulfilled? Learn the promises of your Heavenly Father, dear one, and pray them back to Him. Watch His heart move toward you and move your heart toward Him.

One last note, and then we will pack it up for the day and take a break from all this heavy lifting. Check out James 5:13–18.

10. What makes prayer effective, according to James?

_____

_____

_____

_____

11. What stood out to you most in James's instructions on how we ought to pray?

_____

_____

_____

12. How will you begin implementing the things we've learned today?

_____

_____

_____

My own hope and prayer is that you begin seeking out the promises of your Beloved in His Word and allow Him to wash over you with His tenderness. I pray that you will cry out to Him and call Him out on all that His has promised. Then in faith, sit quietly, wait patiently, and watch Him move heaven and earth to answer your call. It is an incredible thing.

Oswald Chambers, on Prayer:

Our prayers are heard, not because we are in earnest, not because we suffer, but because Jesus suffered.

It will be a wonderful moment for some of us when we stand before God and find that the prayers we clamoured for in early days and imagined were never answered, have been answered in the most amazing way, and that God's silence has been the sign of the answer. If we always want to be able to point to something and say, This is the way God answered my prayer, God cannot trust us yet with His silence.

Prayer is not getting things from God, that is the most initial stage; prayer is getting into perfect communion with God; I tell Him what I know He knows in order that I may get to know it as He does.

I am perfectly confident that the [woman] who does not spend hours alone with God will never know the anointing of the Holy Spirit. The world must be left outside until God alone fills the vision…God has promised to answer prayer. It is not that He is unwilling, for the fact is, He is more willing to give than we are to receive. But the trouble is, we are not ready.

Never make the blunder of trying to forecast the way God is going to answer your prayer.

Inarticulate prayer, the impulsive prayer that looks so futile, is the thing God always heeds. The habit of ejaculatory prayer ought to be the persistent habit of each one of us.

A most beneficial exercise in secret prayer before the Father is to write things down exactly so I see exactly what I think and want to say. Only those who have tried these ways know the ineffable benefit of such strenuous times in secret.

By intercessory prayer we can hold off Satan from other lives and give the Holy [Spirit] a chance with them. No wonder Jesus put such tremendous emphasis on prayer.

Faith is deliberate confidence in the character of God whose ways you may not understand at the time.

If God sees that my spiritual life will be furthered by giving the things for which I ask, then He will give them, but that is not the end of prayer. The end of prayer is that I come to know God Himself.

Whenever the insistence is on the point that God answers prayer, we are off the track. The meaning of prayer is that we get hold of God, not of the answer.

Get into the habit of saying, "Speak, Lord," and life will become a romance. [25]

I am so proud of you for sticking this one out with me. I know this week has been extremely challenging, but I pray it has also been a blessing. I know that we have trodden into some muddy trenches; ones which you probably didn't want to have to drudge through. Maybe you're still struggling to get your boots unstuck. Maybe walking through some of these topics has brought you into yet another valley after you had been sitting on some hilltops. That's okay. This is a process and a journey. We may walk through dark low points, but we know that our King is walking right there with us. We know that He will carry us to the next hilltop and beyond.

As we close out this week, I want to return to our theme psalm and remember all the great promises the Lord has given us in it. Let's begin to memorize these verses and pray them back to Him in our times of trouble, strife, stress, weakness, and fear. When we're angry and frustrated that so much time has passed, while we're still wondering if our wounds are ever really going to heal, and when we're tired of trying and waiting, let's remember that our Redeemer remains at our side, whispering tenderly to us. He says to pray and believe.

I sought the Lord, and He answered me,

And delivered me from all my fears.

They looked to Him and were radiant,

And their faces will never be ashamed.

This poor (girl) cried, and the Lord heard (her)

And saved (her) out of all (her) troubles.

The angel of the Lord encamps around those who fear Him,

And rescues them.

O taste and see that the Lord is good;

How blessed is the (daughter) who takes refuge in Him!

(Psalm 34:4–8)

Week 3

God Provides
Psalm 34:9–10

Recall that as we began last week, I said the journey was going to get harder before it got easier, and man, it did. It got rough, didn't it? Well, I think this week, we may begin our journey back up toward some new hilltops. Though I can't promise we won't hit another valley or two before we complete this thing, I am so excited to start in on this week's lesson.

I think that we will get to see some real progress forward in our hearts and circumstances. However, I know that some things will still be difficult to address as we move from inward reflections and changes of our own hearts to dealing with our husbands and confronting some things alongside them. Tighten up your hiking boots girl, put a psalm in your heart, let a prayer be in your mouth, and let's start climbing.

DAY 1: THOSE WHO FEAR THE LORD LACK NO GOOD THING

The Lord is near to all who call upon Him, To all who call upon Him in truth. He will fulfill the desire of those who fear Him; He will also hear their cry and will save them. (Psalm 145:18–19)

A couple of times, we have discussed the things that enable our prayers to be heard. We are to seek first the kingdom of God, be fervent and thankful in our prayers, and most importantly, we are to have *faith* that our King will answer us. Today we are going to look at the gifts our gracious Provider desires to lavish upon us and the ways that they will aid in our healing.

Let's start by looking at our Psalm 34. Read verses 9 and 10.

1. When we fear the Lord, we lack

> a. Only the things we want
>
> b. Joy and Peace for our heartaches
>
> c. Blessings
>
> d. No *good* thing

2. What good things do you feel that you currently lack?

_____

_____

_____

_____

Let's look at some of the directions our King has given to us with regard to seeking Him and asking for the good things that He has promised us.

Read and respond to Psalm 146.

3. What stood the most in this passage?

_____

_____

_____

_____

Did you notice how many times it said, "the LORD"? I find this very intriguing. That phrase alone is enough to make us pause and think, *All of this is in the perfect hands of the King, and nothing has escaped His control.*

But look also at what the writer says he is going to do. "I will praise the Lord all my life; I will sing praise to my God as long as I live" (verse 2 NIV). He doesn't give any indication that his praise is going to cease in the instance of sorrow or turmoil, does he? In fact, the implication is just the opposite. He is praising God *all* his life.

My sweet friend, you don't have to be happy to praise the Lord. You don't have to *feel* like praising in order to praise the Lord. Sometimes it takes an act of obedience to cry out to the Father and thank Him for all that He has already done and worship Him for what you choose to believe He will continue to do. Your King knows that sometimes it is a sacrifice to praise Him, and He won't condemn you for it if you're honest with Him. What He will do is use your obedience to begin to turn your heart. You will become more and more willing to praise, and it will become more and more of a response of gratitude and awe.

As we return to our psalm, let's look again at the person we are to put our trust in. It is not in princes (husbands) or in any other human. I don't put my trust in my mom, my boss, the government, my friends, or my children. Remember, dear one, we are making a choice to love and honor our Jesus by believing that He will heal us and restore our marriages. We don't remain in this relationship to retain our pride, please our parents, or protect our children. All those reasons will fail us.

We must come to the point where we decide to stay and remain faithful because we believe Jesus has asked us to do so. That is our *one* reason, and that is reason enough. We put our trust in *Him*. We believe Him, regardless of what our husbands do or don't do and regardless of what our parents, friends, or church family think. We pray and plead in faith because we believe and hope in Jesus and Him alone.

In Psalm 146, the psalmist says that every person of flesh and blood will return to the earth and that our plans will become nothing. All the expectations of future thrills during a special vacation, the house that was to be purchased, and the college that was to be attended simply vanish when he or she no longer walks the dust of the earth.

"But the plans of the Lord stand firm forever, the purposes of his heart through all generations" (Psalm 33:11 NIV). Read that one again. Your plans, my plans, and our husbands' plans fail and are caught up into the mist, but "the plans of the Lord stand firm forever." How encouraging is that?

Look with me one more time at Psalm 146, then we'll move on. Note what the writer says in verse 9, about watching over strangers or foreigners. Do you ever feel like a foreigner or a stranger in your own home? Have you felt like your husband's behavior has made your children feel fatherless or made you feel husbandless?

4. Respond to what the Lord says to you in verse 9.

_____

_____

_____

_____

As a military wife, I often lack a husband to help make decisions, plan the educational direction for our children, and enjoy conversation and friendship with. I have had to learn repeatedly that Jesus is my husband. He is the One to whom I run when I am lonely, sad, or frustrated. He is the One I trust with all the big decisions that I have to make in my husband's absence. Though I'm not actually a widow and my children aren't truly fatherless, sometimes we feel as though we are. Sometimes our geographic circumstances make it such that we must operate without a man in the house.

I remember how the circumstances leading up to my husband's affair made me often feel widowed or as though I (or he) was a stranger in our home. But my King has continually and faithfully shown up to be the hero in my story and proven that He "watches over [me] and sustains the fatherless and the [husbandless]" (verse 9 NIV). In the midst of your trial, you have the wisdom and counsel of the Lord and His power to change you and your circumstances. You have His goodness, mercy, love, forgiveness, and provision.

> *Now the God of peace, who brought back from the dead that great shepherd of the sheep, our Lord Jesus, by the blood of the everlasting agreement, equip you thoroughly for the doing of his will! May he effect in you everything that pleases him through Jesus Christ, to whom be glory for ever and ever. (Hebrews 13:20–21, Phillips)*

5. Write down what God is going to do for you by the blood of the covenant ("agreement" in this translation).

_____

_____

_____

_____

Did you say, "Equip me thoroughly for the doing of His will"? I hope so. Think for a moment about what you *know* God's will is for you. There are some basic scriptural principles that apply to all of us, all the time. As we saw last week for example, we are all told to love our husbands and children. We know we are to respect those in authority over us. We are directed to be thankful and pray at all times. Tell the Lord the things that you know you should do but have a difficult time accomplishing. Now write them down, completing this sentence:

6. Father, I trust you to equip me to do your will in

_____

_____

_____

_____

As we have seen already, your King will not only equip you to do all that He has asked of you but will also give you the peace that you need to walk it out.

7. Write Psalm 55:16–19 in your own words.

_____

_____

_____

_____

While I was in the midst of the war that had been waged against my marriage, the psalms were so precious to me. Time and time again, David speaks of his life being in danger, his soul being war-torn, and all the enemies that stood against him.

It was medicine to my soul to cry and beat my chest along with him, to plead for justice, and to ask for God's hand of judgment to fall upon the woman who had ensnared my husband with her evil enticements. It was also so precious to see that in Psalm 55, David's heart moved from fear and anger to peace and trust in his God. Just look at the change from what he says in verse 15 to his words in verse 18.

> *Let death take my enemies by surprise; let them go down alive to the realm of the dead, for evil finds lodging among them [Can you relate? I can.] … He will redeem my soul in peace from the battle which is against me, For they are many who strive with me.*

Isn't it so encouraging that we are not the only ones who have wished death on those who have caused our pain? Isn't it even more encouraging that Jesus redeems our souls in peace from many things that contend with us? He redeems us from our spiritual enemy, our *perceived* physical enemy (the other woman), and from our biggest enemy: our own mind, which plagues us with fears, doubts, and insecurities. It is so comforting to know that my Savior also understands all the anger, hurt, and vengeance that whirls inside my mind.

Reflect on Hebrews 4:14–16 a little while.

8. Jesus sympathizes with our _____, and He has been _____ in all the _____ that you and I have.

9. Write down some of your weaknesses and temptations with regard to your current circumstance.

_____

_____

_____

_____

Has it ever occurred to you that Jesus also battled those same demons? He too dealt with enemies, betrayers, and mockers. He wanted to quit. Remember the Garden of Gethsemane? (see Matthew 26:36–46) Didn't He plead with the Father for another way? He was tempted to look for an easy escape from His circumstances, just as you and I have been.

Jesus has been angry and brokenhearted, just like you and I have been (see Mark 11:15–18 and John 11:30–35). Don't think for a minute that Satan wasn't right there with Him in some of those circumstances, whispering in His ear, as his demons do to us, saying, *You know you want to hate them. Just look how horribly they have treated you. You know they'll never change. You should just give up now and get out while you can.*

What do you think the temptation on the mountaintop in Matthew 4:8 was about? Satan was offering Jesus a way to gain the world without having to face the cross. Satan is a liar of course, but that's the point. He was promising Jesus an easier way to buy back humanity so that He wouldn't have to bear the agony that He knew was coming. But in His mercy, the King didn't give up on us. He made a way so that we might walk through our circumstances with strength and courage. He made a way so that we might smile again. Just read Psalm 39:7–13.

> *But now, Lord, what do I look for? My hope is in you. Save me from all my transgressions; do not make me the scorn of fools. I was silent; I would not open my mouth, for you are the one who has done this. Remove your scourge from me; I am overcome by the blow of your hand. When you rebuke and discipline anyone for their sin, you consume their wealth like*

a moth— surely everyone is but a breath. Hear my prayer, Lord, listen to my cry for help; do not be deaf to my weeping. I dwell with you as a foreigner, a stranger, as all my ancestors were. Look away from me, that I may enjoy life again before I depart and am no more. (NIV)

I know it's hard to understand that these circumstances are gifted to us by the hand of the Almighty, without getting angry with Him for allowing us to be hurt. However, we must remember that even our suffering is a gift through which the gentle, loving hand of our Father moves us into deeper intimacy with Himself.

So when we read this passage, we can scream along with David, "Remove your scourge from me. Do not make me the scorn of fools. Do not be deaf to my weeping." My favorite part, is, "Turn Your gaze away from me, that I may smile again" (NASB). Wouldn't it be wonderful to have the heavy hand of our circumstance removed so that we could simply enjoy life and smile again as these translations say?

It's okay to cry out to your Jesus, my friend. It's okay to blame Him and let your anger fall on His shoulders. But be like David, and let His tender hands wipe the tears from your cheeks and caress your head. Let Him brush the hair from your face and whisper in your ear, *I will never leave you or forsake you.* (see Hebrews 13:5)

Forever Reign[26]

By Jason Ingram, Reuben Morgan
You are love You are love
On display for all to see
You are light You are light
When the darkness closes in
You are hope You are hope
You have covered all my sin
You are peace You are peace
When my fear is crippling

10. I'll give you a moment to cry out to the Lord. Rewrite Psalm 39 as a prayer to Jesus about your circumstances.

_____

_____

_____

_____

    I want to leave you today with the reminder that not only will God give you all that you need to bring wholeness and healing to your heart and marriage as you cry out to Him but also that He is all that you need. *He* is the very *essence* of *all* that you need. Look at one last passage as you consider the mercy of our King to provide all to those who ask Him.

11. According to Hebrews 13:5–6, we do not need to covet (desire or lust over) anything because

_____

_____

_____

_____

I hope it brings great encouragement and peace to your heart to know that no matter what the circumstance, how low the valley is, or how deep the wound is, your gracious Redeemer stands right beside you and provides for all your needs: finances, courage, patience, and peace. *He* is *all* that you need. May He go before you today and lead you into deeper faith and intimacy with Himself.

DAY 2: THE LORD PROVIDES OPPORTUNITIES TO BE OURSELVES

O Lord, You have searched me and known me. You know when I sit down and when I rise up; You understand my thought from afar ... You have enclosed me behind and before, And laid Your hand upon me. (Psalm 139:1–2, 5)

I am excited that you've joined me today, although as I look at this chapter's content, I am wrestling in my spirit with how to approach it. I know this will be a challenging study for us, but I hope it will be sweet and refreshing as well.

By this point in our journey, we have no doubt encountered many valleys and shed many tears, but today, our precious King wants to remind us of how valuable we are and how much He cares for our human needs and weaknesses. He wants us to see that our husbands are working to care for those needs as well. In order for proper healing to take place, we and our husbands must work together to meet each other's needs and provide encouragement and value to each other.

Yesterday, we saw that Jesus provides all that we need and that in Him, we lack no good thing. One of the first things to leave us after our beloveds have betrayed us is our sense of value. Our minds plague us with thoughts like, *Does he really love me? I am so much less than what he wants or needs.* They torment us like a cancer. The need to compare ourselves to the other woman overwhelms our thoughts, and we feel that we can never measure up or be what she is or was.

Maybe we didn't have a deep sense of value to begin with. We always compared ourselves to others and felt inadequate, even before this wound. In either case, we feel so devalued and ashamed that it's very difficult to see how important it is to be treated with respect. Maybe we feel so neglected, betrayed, and abused that we are screaming on the inside, *Why have I allowed such disrespect? I will never allow myself to be made the fool again.* Maybe it's because all of the above thoughts find themselves swirling around in a mixture of confused uncertainties in our minds.

Take a few moments with me today to remind yourself of how valuable you truly are. Return to Matthew 6:26–30, and let's look at our worth in the eyes of Jesus.

1. According to verse 29, who or what is clothed more gloriously than Solomon (the richest, most elegant king ever to walk the earth)?

_____

_____

_____

_____

2. What becomes of these glorious things, which God has clothed so majestically?

_____

_____

_____

_____

3. Who is valued more than they are?

_____

_____

_____

_____

Pause for a moment and think of the fields of wildflowers you've seen, whether in pictures or out on a hike through a mountain meadow. Aren't they absolutely stunning? Don't they make you just want to lie down right in the middle of them and stay all day soaking up their beauty? Don't you long to relish in their joy as they sweetly dance in the gentle breeze?

This is how your King sees you. This is what He made you to be to the world. You are made to be the image of the beauty, tranquility, and joy of the Creator. You are designed to be a reflection of His majesty (as in a mirror). Let that sink in for a moment. You are made to display the majesty and beauty of the Creator God, just as those fields of flowers were made to display His glory.

Genesis tells us, "God created man in His own image, in the image of God He created him; male and female He created them ... Whoever sheds man's blood, By man his blood shall be shed, For in the image of God He made man" (Genesis 1:27; 9:6). Have you ever thought about the fact that you are the very image of God? Does this really hit you in the face? Wow! We bear the very personhood of God in our human bodies. How incredible is that!

God proclaimed that if someone were to kill another person, her own life would be required of her. What this means to us is that God values us, and our lives are precious to Him. We ought to value each other's lives. We are to see those around us as bearers of the image of the Almighty and to value them as such. In so doing, we need to be careful to see ourselves in that way too.

It is important that we learn who God has made us and to become that woman, rather than striving to be the person someone else (including our husbands) expects of us. We should not be pursuing some image that we have crafted in our own minds (an image more like the other woman perhaps). After all, she is so much more _____ than us, right? No. The women we are on the inside and the unique personality that our Creator has placed within us are who we need to rediscover and simply *be*. We most reflect Jesus and His character when we are ourselves, not when we are striving to change our personhood. As image bearers, our unique personalities require respect and honor, not because we deserve it or are somehow superior to others, but simply because God commanded it.

As you think about that today, let's do a little exercise. This is not a study of scriptures per se, although the concepts are biblical. I want us to take a few moments to do some soul-searching because it is important that we learn to give ourselves boundaries and consequences if someone disrespects our boundaries. What I mean by boundaries is that you create expectations for how you want the people around you to treat you and how you will respond if they do not.

Dr. Henry Cloud and Dr. John Townsend say in *Boundaries in Marriage* that you cannot put boundaries on another person but can put them on yourself.[27] Their principle explains that if a person (your husband, your children, or someone at the grocery store) crosses your boundaries, you will have a response prepared that will help you communicate your disapproval. You should either remove yourself from the situation to regroup, or respectfully say that it is not okay with you that the other person has said this or that and that there are consequences for it. The consequences for a particular boundary should be decided in advance so that you don't respond in anger but instead speak with love and quietness of soul. It is imperative that consequences be respectfully stated and acted upon.

For example, you might have asked your husband to give you advance notice when he needs your attention to discuss something after he arrives home from work. However, he walks into the house and begins making demands without regard for what you are doing. You may simply say, "I cannot discuss this right now. I am in the middle of something," and proceed to go about what you are doing. However, if he has notified you that he needs to speak with you, you need to be sure to set aside the time and prepare yourself so that you may be attentive to him when he arrives. Now it's your turn.

4. What are some ways that you have felt disrespected or devalued in your marriage?

_____

_____

_____

_____

5. What boundaries can you set around yourself to correct this?

_____

_____

_____

_____

It will require some planning and learning about yourself and your needs within the relationship to fully grasp what your boundaries need to be, but you're on the right track by just writing down a few them. Establishing boundaries will also require you to express your expectations to your husband, which brings us to another very important step in healing our marriages and our own personhood.

I once heard it said that disappointment is simply unmet expectations. These disappointments may be real or imagined, but they are disappointments nonetheless. Often, we do not discuss our expectations with others. We simply place them on people and then become disgruntled when they don't live up to what we had hoped or planned. It automatically sets them up for failure. When they fail, we begin the blame cycle. In your situation and mine, we may even begin to drag out the wound and the old sins, which we were supposed to have forgiven.

One example would be when you expect your husband to buy you an extravagant birthday gift, but you tell him not to get you anything. Your husband, trying to be a good man who wants to please his wife, buys nothing. You then get angry. Why does this happen? Because your expectation has not been met. Forgive my directness, but you expected him to ignore your false humility and buy you something that would express his undying love and gratitude to you. You again falsely assumed that he doesn't truly care for you as you'd hoped because he didn't go out and buy the flowers or an expensive necklace.

Men do not see the world as you and I do. Your husband feels that he has done a good thing by not purchasing a gift because that's what you asked of him, but you feel slighted and unvalued. Do you see what I mean? If you expect your husband to buy you a gift, tell him so. Don't set him up for failure. Don't expect him to read your mind or value the same things that you value (i.e. flowers, chocolate, or random surprises).

I promise you that if the two of you are still walking this thing out together, and he wants to maintain your marriage, it means he truly values you. He may not express it the way you want him to because he is a different personality. Stop playing games with him and learn to share your thoughts and expectations. After all, he's just a man—a human man. He's not Jesus.

6. Let's look at a couple of Proverbs to help us solidify these principles in our minds.

Proverbs 11:16

"A _____ woman attains honor."

Proverbs 10:19

"When there are many words, transgression is unavoidable, But [she] who _____ [her] lips is wise."

Proverbs 13:12

"Hope deferred [unmet expectations] makes the heart _____, But desire fulfilled is a tree of _____."

Proverbs 12:25

"Anxiety in a [woman's] heart _____ it down, But a _____ word makes it glad."

Proverbs 20:5

"A plan in the heart of a [person] is like deep _____, But a [woman] of understanding _____ it out."

I love the last one because I think it goes two ways. If you are wise, you will express your expectations and enable others to respond appropriately so that you will avoid setting them up for failure. You will also seek out the thoughts and plans of others so that you can appropriately address their concerns. This wise practice creates trust and understanding between both parties and ultimately increases the feeling of value and intimacy between them.

Along with the loss of value in our relationships, we sometimes lose ourselves completely in the midst of great trauma. In many of the marriages I have seen, the wife's sense of self has been lost long before the betrayal by her husband. The constant wearing out of her soul by the abuse, lack of respect, or emotional isolation, diminishes her own personhood little by little until she is as a wilted, dried-out flower whose petals are falling to the floor. I was one such person. I was so wrapped up in my husband, my children, and all that was *them* that I had forgotten who I was and what *I* loved.

Now, I need to pause a moment to give a disclaimer. I do not believe in pampering one's self because one deserves it. We must be careful not to become self-absorbed and self-centered as we seek to pursue our own interests. There is a delicate balance in this, as with all aspects of life.

We need the Holy Spirit to guide and correct us as we seek to maintain a correct perspective. We are sinful creatures who deserve only hell, thus we don't pamper ourselves because we are worth it, as the world might say. Rather, Jesus, in His unfathomable *grace*, gave us heaven *and* the opportunity to enjoy life on this earth and to be blessed in our activities while we dwell in it. As He said, "I came that they may have life, and have it abundantly" (John 10:10).

Jesus has given us the command to care for our bodies, spirits, and minds. That command is our motivation today.

7. What does Ecclesiastes 8:15 say about the days given to us by God?

_____

_____

_____

_____

Proverbs 4:23 says, "Guard your heart above all else, for it is the source of life" (HCSB). This means that we need to be careful what we spend our thoughts and emotions on. Jesus purchased life for us—both future and present life. He has given us freedom to enjoy life and maintain that joy in our hearts. That includes pursuing the things that bring us joy—the things that are just our own and no one else's.

Your Creator has made you uniquely you, and no one else can be the woman that He has made you to be. No one can fill the role that He has made you to fill. Every so often, take some time to discover whom Jesus made you to be and the passions that He has placed inside of you. Ask yourself, *What are the things I've always said I wanted to do, see, and experience? Who are the people I enjoy spending time with? What are the things I've wished I could do but haven't had time or the opportunity to do so? Of these things, what might I be able to make time to pursue?*

Perhaps you need to get alone, take a long walk, or grab a cup of coffee and sit on a park bench. Maybe you need to fill the tub and soak or pick up a long-forgotten paintbrush.

Recently, a friend asked me what my hobbies were. I had to take a few moments to think. My initial reaction was, *Who has time for hobbies?* I began to ponder, *What is the thing I enjoy most when I am able to make time for it?* The one thing that came to mind was my writing. I love to write. I enjoy being an author, but more than that, I love to use my penmanship skills. I relish the feeling of a perfectly weighted pen in my hand as it strokes a crisp piece of paper. I get a deep sense of satisfaction from feeling the keys of a computer keyboard depress beneath my fingertips and from watching the words appear like magic, filling the void of the screen.

My favorite form of writing is crafting love notes or cards of encouragement to my children and my girlfriends (I sometimes write them to my husband, but he's not often a word person). When I had a less complicated life, I used pray for my friends and then write the prayers and a scripture on a card and drop them in the mail just to bless them. I've lost that pleasure with the busyness of life, but my friend challenged me to pick it up again.

I have to tell you, it is so life giving to be an encouragement to others. I pray that you can find something you love that will also breathe life into those around you. Whatever you love to do, do it, and do it unto the Lord.

8. What does Colossians 3:23–24 say in regard to what we've just talked about?

_____

_____

_____

_____

9. Go ahead and take time to write down some of the things that you enjoy and would like to find time to pursue.

_____

_____

_____

_____

Today is a good day to start planning to pursue those things. It might be helpful to ask a family member or a close friend to watch the kids for a couple of hours. You may need to ask your husband to help you carve out time in your schedules or plan a little extra money in the budget to get away (We'll talk more about expenses later).

It is also important to plan time with your girlfriends. I have found it to be very refreshing and exhilarating to my soul to have a ladies' night every few weeks. My husband is wonderful, and he *is* my *best* friend, but he isn't a girl, and he can't be what my girlfriends are to me. A ladies' Bible study, a book club, or an art night are great ways to enjoy relationships and be refreshed. Fellowship with godly women who are pursuing Jesus alongside us can be lifesaving, especially when we're in the midst of a difficult journey.

10. What does Hebrews 10:23–25 say about our time with friends?

_____

_____

_____

_____

11. According to Ecclesiastes 4:12, two are better than one, and three are better still. Why is this true?

_____

_____

_____

_____

If you don't have any ladies whom you call close friends, who love Jesus and love you, and in whom you can confide your current struggles, please take time right now to pray that God will bring some to you. Remember, He has already promised that you would lack no good thing. He knows you need encouragement and camaraderie with godly sisters. Ask Him right now, and ask Him tomorrow, the next day, and the next, until He brings them to you.

Then go out, enjoy a cup of coffee or a glass of wine with some good conversation, and laugh. Let them make you laugh. We girls love to have silly conversations and giggle. From age two to ninety-two, we love to find things that make us laugh. Ask your girlfriends to help you learn to laugh again.

It is important to laugh with your husband as well. Laughter is amazing medicine. In the midst of the darkest part of our deepest valleys and at the recommendation of another couple who had also walked the same valleys, my husband and I began to watch standup comedy. It was so deeply healing to sit next to each other and laugh. It rebuilt bonds and released tension. It gave us something to look forward to each weekend while we were still struggling to enjoy time together without harsh words or anger.

12. Read and write what the following passages speak to you.

Job 8:20–22

_____

_____

_____

_____

Psalm 126:1–6

_____

_____

_____

_____

I know this has been a long day, and I talked a lot, but I pray that it has been of some benefit to you. I'm so grateful for your patience and your diligence to stick it out with me as we continue down this road. I pray that you allow the things we've learned today to seep into your soul and cause you to see that you are not only an individual worthy of expressing yourself in your own unique ways but also that you are valued by God, and you are a bearer of His image.

DAY 3: THE LORD PROVIDES SLEEP AND REFRESHMENT

I will both lie down in peace, and sleep; For You alone,
O Lord, make me dwell in safety. (Psalm 4:8)

Spiritual, emotional, and mental health are key to our healing, but we also need to care for our bodies. They are the temple of the Holy Spirit, remember? Whether we like it or not, our bodies, minds, and spirits need restfulness, sleep, refreshing, and food. It can be extremely exhausting to fight this battle for our marriages. Often, rest and the ability to eat well elude us. Remember that our God has promised not to withhold good things from us. We all know that sleep and refreshment are good things. Food is a *good* thing. However, we may find it very challenging to enjoy some or all of these blessings.

Oswald Chambers says those seemingly small things like eating and sleeping are very important to keeping our spirits alive, particularly when we are depressed or struggling through a trial. First Kings 19:5 tells of the prophet Elijah suffering a great depression and hiding from those who sought his life. An angel told him to "Arise and eat." Chambers says of this,

> If human beings were not capable of depression, we would have no capacity for happiness and exaltation. There are things in life that are designed to depress us; for example, things that are associated with death. Whenever you examine yourself, always take into account your capacity for depression.

> When the Spirit of God comes to us, He does not give us glorious visions, but He tells us to do the most ordinary things imaginable. Depression tends to turn us away from the everyday things of God's creation. But whenever God steps in, His inspiration is to do the most natural, simple things—things we would never have imagined God was in, but as we do them we find Him there. The inspiration that comes to us in this way is an initiative against depression. But we must take the first step and do it in the inspiration of God. If, however, we do something simply to

overcome our depression, we will only deepen it. But when the Spirit of God leads us instinctively to do something, the moment we do it the depression is gone. As soon as we arise and obey we enter a higher plane of life.[28]

I think it is important for us to remember that depression is normal. It is a human response to the terribly broken world we live in. Look back at Isaiah 53 again for a moment. Notice the depression in the life of Jesus.

1. According to Isaiah 53:3–4, Jesus was (Circle all that apply)

Approved by all people	Esteemed and appreciated
A man of sorrows	Full of joy and excitement
One from whom people hide their faces	Acquainted with grief
Despised and rejected	Stricken and afflicted

I don't know about you, but that sounds rather depressing to me. Our Jesus not only knows our sorrows intimately, but verse 4 says that He bore them in His own body and spirit. That means that you and I do not have to remain in a state of deep sorrow and depression. He bore our grief in His own body so that we don't have to. It's not healthy to remain in a state of sleeplessness or to go without food. As Chambers says, sometimes we simply need to do the natural, simple things and find God in them. He will gently lead us out of our depression and into joy as we seek to honor Him with our minds, spirits, and bodies.

Compare Isaiah 35:10, Isaiah 51:11, and John 16:20–22.

2. What do all these say about your current depression?

_____

_____

_____

_____

Often when we are depressed, sleep eludes us because our minds are consumed with our fears, sorrows, regrets, and desires. We must have peace and quietness in our souls so that our minds can rest. Continue praying for peace of mind and for God to guard your heart. As we have learned, sometimes it takes bringing the thing before our Redeemer over and over.

If you're having trouble sleeping because you can't get a certain thought out of your mind, get up and read your Bible. You're not sleeping anyway. Pray for the Holy Spirit to give you a verse to memorize and pray over. He will. He promises that He will (see Hebrews 4:12). Then go back to bed with that passage in mind, pray it back to the Father over and over, and repeat it to yourself again and again—out loud if possible. Look at what the Bible says we ought to be doing with these thoughts that keep us from sleep.

> *Do not be anxious about anything, but in every situation, by prayer and petition, with thanksgiving, present your requests to God. And the peace of God, which transcends all understanding, will guard your hearts and your minds in Christ Jesus.* (Philippians 4:6–7 NIV)

3. What will the peace that transcends understanding do?

_____

_____

_____

_____

The peace of God, which surpasses all our capabilities of understanding our present and future circumstances, will guard our hearts and minds against the constant nagging of evil thoughts. Whether we are planning revenge, pondering what we would do in a given situation, or plaguing ourselves with images and memories, the peace of our King transcends them all.

4. According to Hebrews 4:8–11, true rest comes from where?

_____

_____

_____

_____

The writer of Hebrews wants us to understand that heaven, or rather eternity, is our rest. However, he says that we are to be "diligent to enter that rest," which tells us that our hope of peace and rest is for here on Earth. Let me say it *again*. We have access to the deep, all-encompassing, perfect peace of heaven here on Earth *while* we yet live among the death and destruction of this world.

How deeply we experience that rest, however, is directly related to our faith in Jesus. We must live by faith, believing that He will keep us in perfect peace. We must be purposeful in *seeking out* His rest and then committing our minds to dwell in it. It is a discipline. We must be diligent in asking for His peace to cover our thoughts. Most importantly, we need to use His Word to give us the power to fight off those "arguments and every high thing that exalts itself against the knowledge of God" and to bring "every thought into captivity to the obedience of Christ" (2 Corinthians 10:5 NKJV).

Interestingly enough, the verse immediately following the command in Hebrews 4 (to be diligent to enter God's rest) tells us that the Word of God gets our thoughts to where they ought to be. Hebrews 12:4 says,

> *For the word of God is living and powerful, and sharper than any two-edged sword, piercing even to the division of soul and spirit, and of joints and marrow, and is a discerner of the thoughts and intents of the heart"* (emphasis mine).

In other words, it is by the living breathing power of God's Word that we are able to cast down the evil thoughts, temptations, and bitter resentments that keep us up at night. The sharpness of scripture cuts away at the hidden places of our souls, leaving only what is true, noble, right, pure, lovely, admirable, excellent, and praiseworthy (see Philippians 4:8 NIV).

5. What are some of the things that keep you up at night?

_____

_____

_____

_____

6. Take a moment to write a prayer to your King, laying those things at the foot of the cross.

_____

_____

_____

_____

As we continue in the obedience to make His Word our source of hope and peace, let's look at a few more scriptures about sleep.

7. Read and respond to Psalm 4:6–8.

_____

_____

_____

_____

Psalm 127:2 says, "It is vain for you to rise up early, To sit up late, To eat the bread of sorrows; For so He gives His beloved sleep" (NKJV).

8. To whom does God give sleep?

_____

_____

_____

_____

9. Write down what you learn from Jeremiah 31:25–26.

_____

_____

_____

_____

The King grants sleep to His beloved. That's you. If you have been unable to sleep, my friend, begin praying for the Lord to give you rest and make it sweet and refreshing. He knows that you need your rest. It is a *good* thing. His very Word promises that He *will* grant it.

Self-care, as some would call it, is also very necessary when healing from tragedy and for refreshing our bodies and spirits, although I don't really care for the term. Self-care implies self-centeredness, but we must be very purposeful to separate the selfish fulfillment of the flesh with the need to be merciful toward our bodies, minds, and emotions.

Self-centeredness is found mainly in the attitude in which we do a particular thing. It isn't what we do that makes us self-centered but the attitude of self-indulgence that arises when we feel that we deserve it. *After all*, we conclude, *I have put up with quite a lot. Why shouldn't I pamper myself?* However good it may feel at the time, self-centeredness will only produce feelings of entitlement and ultimately, resentment. In it, we are stroking our flesh and coddling our wounds rather than moving toward a gracious healing of our souls.

Conversely, self-care in the sense that we will use it is something done to promote healing and refreshing. I cannot tell you specifically which activities are selfish for you and which are not. Each thing will be different for each person.

I can give you an example from my own life to assist in making a better distinction. For me, going to get my nails done because I want to feel better *about myself* and because I believe I have a *right* to feel pretty is self-indulgent. However, soaking in a long hot bath is refreshing because I can think in the silence and pray without interruption.

For you, the opposite may be true. You may find that going to get a huge cup of coffee feels self-indulgent but getting a massage is calming. The gauge on whether something is self-indulgent is likely going to be whether it draws us closer to Jesus. If we are in a place of humility before Jesus and seeking to be refreshed and restored in our souls, we're in the right spot. If we are in a place of feeling entitled to some sort of reward for all we've endured, we're probably being self-indulgent.

10. Look again at Colossians 3:23. For whom are you working or in this case, refreshing?

_____

_____

_____

_____

Often, time alone in a quiet place to think, pray, cry, and sing is what I needed most during the deepest times of struggle. However, there were also times that a cup of coffee with a good friend was so refreshing to my spirit. Perhaps it may help to do a bit more soul-searching or even experimentation to discover the activity that will best facilitate refreshment for you. Yesterday, do you remember listing the things that you enjoy doing? Continue looking for more opportunities and activities to restore joy and pleasure to your life but also seek your pursuits in a way that is honoring to the Lord.

As Oswald Chambers reminded us at the beginning of today's lesson, it is also important to eat well, even though we may not feel like it. Our bodies require lots of *healthy* calories. Do not use this time of grief as a crash diet, especially if you have been feeling particularly self-conscious about your body. Fasting is good, prayer is absolutely necessary, and food is as well. Fast for a time but then eat.

If you need to make some changes to your body, do so in a healthy manner. Maybe now is a good time to begin reading up on proper nutrition (I highly recommend looking into multiple approaches and not just one philosophy). Putting new, healthier habits into practice is wise, but we must do so in a way that honors the Lord and the body that He has given us. It is not wise for us to diet in a manner that honors only our pride.

We must make plans to nourish our bodies along with our souls. It might also be wise to begin practicing meal planning and preparation. I know this may be difficult because we feel that we don't have the energy or mental focus to plan, but jotting down at least a few meal ideas will help take the pressure off you later. If necessary, ask your husband, your kids, or friends at church for help in making some easy-to-warm meals in advance so that they are available, and will require minimal effort when you are too tired or weary to think about cooking.

There are also a number of downloadable meal-planning apps for your phone or tablet. Many of them have recipes already built into them. They even put the items on your shopping list for you. These are just a few helpful ways to ensure that you and your family are well nourished while you are focusing on putting your life back together.

Psalm 145:15 says that the hand of our Master gives us food. "The eyes of all look to You, And You give them their food in due time." So "Arise and eat," my dear one.

In all of the things we have addressed today, I cannot stress enough how necessary it is for us to ask the Lord to carry us in *each* of our daily challenges. He cares for *every* circumstance in our lives: eating, sleeping, waking, working, and playing. He is present with us in all of them.

Relish these last few verses, then take a couple of moments before you close the book to respond to the Lord in prayer.

> *Then God said, "I give you every seed-bearing plant on the face of the whole earth and every tree that has fruit with seed in it. They will be yours for food."* (Genesis 1:29 NIV)

> *Everything that lives and moves about will be food for you. Just as I gave you the green plants, I now give you everything.* (Genesis 9:3 NIV)

> *It will come about at the end of seventy years that the Lord will visit Tyre [the oppressor] … Her gain … will not be stored up or hoarded, but [it] will become sufficient food and choice attire for those who dwell in the presence of the Lord.* (Isaiah 23:17–18)

You who call on the Lord, give yourselves no rest, and give him no rest till he establishes Israel [insert your name] and makes her the praise of the earth. The Lord has sworn by his right hand and by his mighty arm: "Never again will I give your grain as food for your enemies, and never again will foreigners drink the new wine for which you have toiled; but those who harvest it will eat it and praise the Lord, and those who gather the grapes will drink it in the courts of my sanctuary." (Isaiah 62:6–9 NIV)

And God is able to make all grace abound to you, so that always having all sufficiency in everything, you may have an abundance for every good deed. (2 Corinthians 9:8)

Come to Me, all who are weary and heavy-laden, and I will give you rest. (Matthew 11:28)

Then, because so many people were coming and going that they did not even have a chance to eat, he said to them, "Come with me by yourselves to a quiet place and get some rest." (Mark 6:31 NIV)

"Now therefore, I pray You, if I have found favor in Your sight, let me know Your ways that I may know You, so that I may find favor in Your sight. Consider too, that this nation is Your people." And He said, "My presence shall go with you, and I will give you rest." (Exodus 33:13–14)

Therefore let us draw near with confidence to the throne of grace, so that we may receive mercy and find grace to help in time of need. (Hebrews 4:16)

Thank you, Father,

That You have made us Your royal nation and given us favor because of Jesus. We praise You for considering us and causing Your Spirit to dwell in our hearts. Thank You for giving us plants and living things to eat and rest for our spirits and bodies. Praise You that Jesus said if we come to Him, we will find rest from all that burdens our hearts and will find help in our time of need. We praise You, Father, for promising to establish us and to make us a praise in the earth because of Your great work and power in our lives.

We pray that You will help us to rest in Jesus and trust Your grace to sustain us. Please help us to leave our burdens at Your feet so that we may be able to love our families and serve You fully. Help us to find nourishment for our bodies and sleep for our eyes. In Jesus's name and for your glory, God, we ask. Amen (so be it).

DAY 4: THE LORD PROVIDES FOR OUR FINANCES

For to those who fear Him there is no want. The young lions
do lack and suffer hunger; But they who seek the Lord shall
not be in want of any good thing. (Psalm 34:9–10)

I have to be honest; this is probably my weakest topic. I am far from having figured this one out, but I want to encourage us both through the Word of God that we *can* have victory in the area of finances. God has much to say regarding money, and there is much to be dealt with in this area within the marriage relationship. There can also be a lot of necessary expenses in dealing with issues after a marriage has been damaged.

Let's begin today with prayer, as I hope you do every day. Then we'll tackle this thing together with the faith that our Redeemer will breathe life and freedom into this topic in our marriages.

LORD, God, King of creation,

We recognize that You own all the worlds and that everything was made by You, for You, and for Your glory. We ask that You would use this day to teach us what is right and true and cut away worldly perspectives and former experiences, which may be shaping our understanding. Please teach us to view money with the same eyes that Jesus views it. Help us to be wise as serpents and as innocent as lambs in our approach to the things of this world. In Jesus's name, so that you may be glorified in us. Amen.

Well, shall we empty our hiking boots of the sand and rocks we've picked up along the journey so far and keep climbing? Perhaps approaching the subject of finances is as daunting for you as it is for me. There are many ways a marital betrayal can cause financial strain. I feel compelled to list them, although I'm quite sure it will by no means be an exhaustive list. First and probably most obvious is that pornography can quickly become very expensive. Phone or credit card bills sometimes skyrocket during an affair.

Expenses, which may need to be incurred after the affair, add up as well. Things that we need to help us heal may be cause for additional strain on our budgets as well: counseling, implementing self-care as we talked about this week, date nights, time away to reconnect with our husbands, and a host of other possibilities.

For my husband and me, one such expense was a new wedding ring. I had taken my ring off because as I said to my husband, "You broke your vow to me, which this ring represents. I cannot wear it anymore." He, of course, said nothing at the time, but weeks later, he began to be sorrowful that I was not wearing a ring.

He asked me to put it back on, and I said, "I will wear it for now, but the circumstances have changed, and I feel it is no longer a valid symbol of your commitment to me. If you want me to continue wearing a ring, you need to buy a new one that represents a new love and commitment." He agreed. I wore the old one until the new one was delivered by FedEx (Who knew people actually buy jewelry that way?).

I had designed the new ring and had had part of it custom made based on a ring that I had seen in one of my favorite movies. My husband placed a symbolic meaning on each piece of it. He decided that one ring would represent the past, one the future, and the third, which is actually three rings in one, would represent the present. So, there are a total of five rings. He said the third ring, being three pieces intertwined, was to represent him, me, and Jesus, without whom we could never make it in this life.

When our marriage is intertwined with Jesus, we are a strong cord that is not easily broken, as Ecclesiastes 4:12 tells us. My husband's purposefulness in creating this new ring was and continues to be so very precious and healing to my heart. I made a vow before the Lord to always tell people my story of redemption when they noticed or mentioned my ring. It became an expression of gratitude to God, for allowing me this extravagant purchase, which we really could not afford. It is always such a joy to watch the walls come down in the lives and hearts of others when I open up and share this piece of myself.

I am continually grateful for my ring(s). Yet it took us many months to pay it off. I prayed and prayed for God's grace and provision to put right the area of finances so that we would not continue stacking up debt and that the ring would be worthy of its cost. We still battle with some debt, but my ring is paid off and it has definitely been worth the cost. I can honestly tell you that this book would never have existed if someone hadn't noticed my ring, and I hadn't told her the story. Afterward, she told someone else, who prompted me to begin praying over this project.

I don't tell you all this because I think you should be out ring shopping, but maybe some other form of extreme change or proof of recommitment may be necessary for your marriage. The possibilities are endless. Perhaps you need a new wardrobe that is less revealing and less threatening for your husband. Maybe you need a more modern, feminine, or engaging wardrobe (which is a topic for another day). You may find it necessary to take a week away to regroup and renew your marriage without the distractions of life and kids. It could be that a new bed, house, city, gym, or job is necessary.

There are also other practical expenses like extra protection against questionable content on your Internet, TV, and phones. You might possibly need to implement traveling along with your husband on business trips. I know some of these things sound extreme, but Jesus is an extremist. He said,

> *If your eye causes you to stumble and sin, throw it out [that is, remove yourself from the source of temptation]! It would be better for you to enter the kingdom of God with one eye, than to have two eyes and be thrown into hell.* (Mark 9:47 AMP)

Sometimes we have to take extreme measures to flea temptation or destruction. Joseph *ran* from Potiphar's wife and left his jacket behind, as Genesis 39 tells us. God commanded Hosea to marry a prostitute in order to display how serious He was about Israel's lack of commitment to Himself (see Hosea 1:2). Equally shocking and grotesquely more vivid is the command given to Ezekiel when the Israelites continued in idolatry. "You shall eat it as a barley cake, having baked it in their sight over human dung." I would consider this pretty extreme, wouldn't you?

We ought to be willing to stop at nothing to ensure that we're obeying God and honoring His will in our lives. This is especially true with our finances. We need to be seeking out every aspect of obedience when it comes to how we spend the money the King has entrusted to us.

1. What are the immediate expenses that you foresee needing to be addressed due to your husband's sin?

_____

_____

_____

_____

2. What long-term expenses do you foresee?

_____

_____

_____

_____

Whatever needs to be accomplished to facilitate healing, take it before the Lord. Pray and seek *His* purpose and desire for you and that thing. Several circumstances might need to change so that trust can be restored and healing can come to your marriage. Certainly, my ring was not the only additional expense we incurred over the year or two following the betrayal. If Jesus is in the thing that you are seeking, He will provide for it.

Take some *time* to *carefully* read through and *reflect* on each of these verses. Pay careful attention to the promises of God's provision.

3. Then note what the Holy Spirit teaches you.

Proverbs 13:22

> *A good man leaves an inheritance to his children's children, And the wealth of the sinner is stored up for the righteous.*

_____

_____

_____

_____

1 Timothy 6:7–9

> *For we have brought nothing into the world, so we cannot take anything out of it either. If we have food and covering, with these we shall be content. But those who want to get rich fall into temptation and a snare and many foolish and harmful desires which plunge men [and women] into ruin and destruction. For the love of money is a root of all sorts of evil, and some by longing for it have wandered away from the faith*

and pierced themselves with many griefs. But flee from these things,
you [woman] of God, and pursue righteousness, godliness, faith, love,
perseverance and gentleness.

---

1 Corinthians 16:1–4

Now about the collection for the Lord's people: Do what I told the Galatian
churches to do. On the first day of every week, each one of you should set
aside a sum of money in keeping with your income, saving it up, so that
when I come no collections will have to be made. Then, when I arrive,
I will give letters of introduction to the men you approve and send them
with your gift to Jerusalem. (NIV)

---

2 Corinthians 9:5–8

So I thought it necessary to urge the brethren that they would go on ahead
to you and arrange beforehand your previously promised bountiful gift,
so that the same would be ready as a bountiful gift and not affected
by covetousness. Now this I say, he who sows sparingly will also reap
sparingly, and he who sows bountifully will also reap bountifully. Each
one must do just as he has purposed in his heart, not grudgingly or under
compulsion, for God loves a cheerful giver. And God is able to make all
grace abound to you, so that always having all sufficiency in everything,
you may have an abundance for every good deed.

_____

_____

_____

Philippians 4:19

And my God will supply all your needs according to His riches in glory in Christ Jesus.

_____

_____

_____

Nehemiah 9:15

You provided bread from heaven for them for their hunger, You brought forth water from a rock for them for their thirst, And You told them to enter in order to possess The land which You swore to give them.

_____

_____

_____

Deuteronomy 8:4

Your clothing did not wear out on you, nor did your foot swell these forty years.

_____

_____

_____

_____

Proverbs 16:3

Commit your works to the LORD And your plans will be established.

_____

_____

_____

Proverbs 3:5–6

Trust in the Lord with all your heart, and do not lean on your own understanding. In all your ways acknowledge him, and he will make straight your paths. (ESV)

_____

_____

_____

Joel 2:25–27

Then I will make up to you for the years That the swarming locust has eaten, The creeping locust, the stripping locust and the gnawing locust, My great army which I sent among you. You will have plenty to eat and be satisfied And praise the name of the Lord your God, Who has dealt wondrously with you; Then My people will never be put to shame. Thus you will know that I am in the midst of Israel, And that I am the Lord your God, And there is no other; And My people will never be put to shame.

_____

_____

_____

_____

As I read these passages, I am in awe of the great provision and faithful care of my King. He has blessed me over and over again. He has supplied my physical needs, but more importantly, He has given me a committed love for Himself, a precious understanding of His goodness, a sweet marriage (*not* perfect by any means), a repentant husband (whom I *know* loves me), and children who love Jesus. What else can I ask for? Sometimes healing is more about perspective than the actualization of our expectations. Learning to have a heart of gratitude will move us miles in our journey toward healing.

As we consider how to approach our finances, I am reminded that we must take each desire, want, and need before the throne of God and seek His purpose in it. I am confident that my God *will* supply all my and your physical, spiritual, and emotional needs. He knows the struggles we face and the consequences of our sins—and those of our husbands—and by the blood of His Son, He has caused each sin to be covered by His grace. We may have to work a little harder or spend a little more to pay for the errors, but when we look to Him in every step, God will give us grace, provision, endurance, and courage to recover all that was lost.

God is faithful, dear one. "He who keeps you" will "not allow your foot to slip" (Psalm 121:3).

DAY 5: THE LORD PROVIDES PLEASURE

You will make known to me the path of life; In Your presence is fullness of joy; In Your right hand there are pleasures forever. (Psalm 16:11)

Good job, sweet sister! You have made it through yet another week. Not only are we walking out this struggle to healing and letting the hours and days flow past us as we put distance between ourselves and our wounds but we're also working hard to allow the Holy Spirit to transform our hearts through persistent study. I'm feeling a bit weary yet reinvigorated at the same time.

It seems that every day brings new challenges but also new hope. As we step forward today, we'll likely be walking into another valley. As we descend the hillside of the lighter-hearted things of the week into a much more challenging subject, my hope is that it will bring us quickly back up a pleasant slope—a mountaintop even. Hang in there with me. This one might get a little rocky.

Rather than beat around the bush in embarrassment or excessive modesty, I'm just going to say the word and get it out: sex. Yes, it's the horrible, ugly misuse of this three-letter word that got most of us into this mess, isn't it? I know that for some of us, this topic may be the hardest thing to think about right now. Others are desperate to have someone validate their hearts' desires to be properly reunited with their husbands.

The word sex likely brings about pain, anger, frustration, depression, longing, desire, and passion. We want to leap for joy and scream in disgust when we hear it because of all the emotions and imaginations that flood our minds. I believe that it is the Lord's desire for us to rediscover the truth about this little word, which is packed with meaning—a truth that *He* has designed and implemented for His glory and our pleasure.

It is extremely important for us to remember that sex was *God's* idea. He created it to be *pleasurable* and *enjoyable* for *both* partners. He could have made us as the animals, which seek to procreate without emotional attachment, or like asexual beings, which simply reproduce with no form of mating. But He didn't.

God gave us sex as a form of speaking love and affirmation to each other. Sex was designed to create unity and oneness between two vastly different creatures: a man and a woman. Unfortunately, after there has been distrust and betrayal, it can be very challenging to get back to a place of enjoyment and unity in our sexual experiences. It is very necessary, nonetheless.

Often, it feels counterintuitive to jump right back into bed because we feel as though we need to starve our husbands of their sexual needs (which we may perceive to be more pronounced than our own) and force them to earn back their rights to our bodies. In fact, the opposite is true. While there is a need to rebuild trust and take some time apart to pray, we must ensure that we don't wait too long. There is an intense need to rebuild the spiritual, emotional, and physical unity that has been lost by reuniting our bodies with our husbands.

1. Write down what you discover in the following verses about the Father's perspective on our sexual experiences.

Genesis 2:18–24

_____

_____

_____

_____

Proverbs 5:18–19

_____

_____

_____

_____

Song of Songs 1:1–4

_____

_____

_____

_____

Song of Songs 4:1–11

_____

_____

_____

_____

Song of Songs 5:1

_____

_____

_____

_____

In Genesis, we discover that of all the amazing, beautiful, and intelligent animals in creation, not one of them was suitable for Adam. Only the woman, Eve, was comparable to him. She was—as we are to our men—flesh of his flesh and bone of his bone. We are their flesh-and-bone, body-and-soul partners. Adam and Eve were equally matched and joined together as one, in a way that only the two of them could be. No animal could meet Adam's needs like Eve could. No other creature could bring him such pleasure and fulfillment as she could. None could be joined with him as one flesh.

The second thing we learn in Genesis is that they were naked and unashamed. In the garden, there was joy unlimited, peace unmatchable, and sex uninhibited. What a thrill, exhilaration, and beauty to enjoy nakedness and sensuality with the deepest intimacy, greatest passion, and most pleasure known to humankind. They knew no sin or shame but only pleasure.

Throughout Proverbs and Song of Songs, we see God's continual blessing of excitement and enjoyment. He, the King of creation, speaks of enraptured love, satisfying breasts, kisses sweeter than wine, perfumes, pleasurable aromas of a romantic sexual experience, bodies bared for visual enjoyment, hearts ravished by enticing glances, French kisses delicious as milk and honey, and the satisfaction that comes with appetites that are well satiated. It is clear that God intends for us to be captivated by each other and well fulfilled in our sexual encounters.

2. Prior to your wound, were you living as if sex was a gift of joy and pleasure for both you and your husband? Why or why not?

_____

_____

_____

_____

3. Are you currently living as though sex is a pleasure and a privilege? Why or why not?

_____

_____

_____

_____

4. What do you think needs to change in your mind and heart in order to view sex as a gift?

_____

_____

_____

_____

5. What might you need to discuss with your husband about his attitudes or behaviors that would help you view sex differently?

_____

_____

_____

_____

Many women (both those who have experienced infidelity and those who have not) have been curious about how I handled myself and have asked me, "Don't you think a man should have to prove himself again before reengaging in sex?"

To that, I simply say, "Yes and no. Yes, there must be repentance and a desire for restoration because we need to guard our hearts from being deceived again. And no, we should not withhold sex from him or from ourselves, simply as a punishment or form of penitence." Oddly enough, those who had endured an affair usually agreed that the draw to be reunited with their husbands was very strong. Yet they felt guilty or shameful about it. It felt as if they were somehow betraying themselves.

Let me tell you right now, dear one, you are not betraying yourself when you allow your husband access to your body. Rather, you are honoring the Lord, your husband, *and* your own body by recommitting yourself to the man you pledged to give yourself to for life. Remember the part in your vows that say, "For better or for worse"? Well, this is worse, isn't it? But we made a promise. Something very supernatural takes place within us when we surrender ourselves to each other in an intimate, physical way.

6. Write down what 1 Corinthians 7:3–5 says regarding this matter.

_____

_____

_____

_____

Now I know verses 3–4 were a bit painful to read—excruciating even—but please remember that one wrong does not justify continued wrongs. Let us be the ones to step into grace, mercy, and righteousness and set the standard for honor. Let us seek to recommit ourselves to our husbands, to enjoy them, to be enraptured in their love, and to be engulfed in their arms. Yes, they must relearn how to pursue and win us back, but we must also relearn to respond with excitement and anticipation. It is not only physically necessary, but as Corinthians says, it's spiritually necessary as well.

Most of us have read in one place or another that the male's sex drive is much stronger than that of the female. We don't need to be told again that men think about sex at least a dozen times a day. However, I don't believe that a man's drive is stronger than a woman's drive. We have just been conditioned to respond to it more secretly or not at all for one reason or another.

I think the difference between the male and female sex drives comes from where we experience the feeling of being loved and accepted. Men tend to feel more love and acceptance through sex (Read any Family Life® recommended book to discover this truth), whereas women experience love through words, touch (non-sexual), and affection.

Yet, isn't it interesting that in 1 Corinthians 7:3, Paul addresses the men first, saying, "The husband must fulfill his duty to his wife"? Then he says, "Likewise, also the wife." In other words, the woman is to follow the man's lead in this committing of one's self to her mate. God expects that as those being led, we are to be considered first in the giving and receiving of each other's body. Are you catching this, my friend? They are commanded to give themselves to us. We are the recipients of a dutiful act of obedience. This indicates that you and I have a need, which must be fulfilled by our men.

Likely, our greatest desire is for tender caressing and loving whispers. But following these, don't we melt into the physical pleasures? Our need for physical gratification within sex may be less intense than our husbands,' but it is a *need*. In His Word, God says so. For some of us, the desire for the physical is far stronger than we let on. I always felt like my sex drive was more intensive than my husband's was. I often felt very shamed of that.

The society we live in, the culture, history, and the church have made us feel that sex is for the pleasure of men rather than for the fulfillment of *both* partners. Although my mom tried very hard to dissuade this philosophy, I was still embarrassed of my sexual desire. It was like I should somehow be ashamed of the fact that I enjoyed the God-given gift of my husband's body and the physical pleasure it brought. I longed for the closeness of my man, the intimacy it created between us, as well as the physical enjoyment. I felt alone in this longing because it seemed that none of my friends felt the same way and apparently, neither did my husband—or so I thought.

Feeling like I was never enough for my husband was also a huge struggle for me—never sexy enough, never daring enough, or provocative enough. I spent many nights in tears, feeling rejected and unwanted. I was convinced that he had a deficient sex drive and that I wasn't enough to spark his flame. I struggled to figure out how other women seemed to catch his attention so easily. The fact of the matter was that my husband didn't have a declined sex drive, but it was just misplaced.

In addition to his selfishness and lust for other women, I too was very selfish and demanding regarding what I expected from him within our intimacy. This made him feel undesirable, unappreciated, and apathetic to my requests and advances. I needed to repent of my insecurities, unwarranted shame, selfish demands, and preconceived, misguided expectations of what sex should be. I needed to relax and enjoy myself. After all, Jesus paid for my freedom from sin and shame, and it was a lack of faith and a slap in my Savior's face for me to remain living ashamed and imprisoned by lies.

As you have been reading through all this, maybe you have felt frustrated or ashamed as I did and like your desires are not reciprocated. Trust me in this: You are *not* alone. Let me assure you, dear one, there is *nothing* wrong with you. It may be that your husband is still struggling with guilt, fear, shame, emotional imbalance, or simple insecurity.

Often, predator women find it rather easy to snare an insecure man because they know just where to stroke his ego. That's not to say that you have failed in this, but perhaps, you might pray for some ways to increase your man's confidence. One way might be to simply tell him that you really desire him and need him to pursue you more often. This creates trust and a sense of bonding between both of you, as you each bare a bit of vulnerability in recognizing that you *both need each other* physically. In a nonjudgmental, non-condemning, and non-demanding manner, share what your physical needs are and then *respond* to him when he advances toward you.

Perhaps your thought process is the opposite of mine, and you feel very detached from your physical desires. It may be that you're feeling ashamed or guilty for not being physically interested in your husband. There could be any number of reasons why you're struggling to desire physical closeness with your husband (other than the obvious issues that come as a result of the betrayal, which we will discuss in a bit). I am no expert, but here are some but certainly not all of the reasons that I have seen women struggle in regard to desiring intimacy.

---

*Lack of trust *Lack of emotional intimacy *Misplaced expectations *Unmet expectations *Sinful lust (which can manifest in sensual movies, novels, and music, pornography, or desiring your mate to be more like someone else) *Hormone or chemical imbalances (Please read up on the diet's influence on this) *Body image struggles *Guilt *Fear *Unwanted pregnancy *Motherhood *Fatigue *Lack of romance outside of the bedroom *Grief *A demanding husband *Martial dysfunction *Poor sexual communication *Past or present abuse *Selfishness *Distrust *Distraction *Busyness *Sexual Disillusionment

---

If these reasons or any other is holding you in captivity, let me remind you that Jesus came to set us free of our guilt and shame. He has also set us free of our failures and disappointments. Perhaps you need to ask Him to take the guilt, shame, dissatisfaction, or disappointments from your heart and enable you to respond positively to your husband's requests.

7. Take a moment to write a prayer to your Redeemer about your struggles.

_____

_____

_____

_____

For some of us, the reality of our husbands' physical needs can be extremely difficult, for no other reason than the fact that our wounds are too deep. We've learned that our husbands are supposed to fulfill their duty to us first, acting as the example and selflessly meeting our needs, but we struggle with the fact that they have not been the warrior heroes that we needed them to be. Thus, we feel it impossible to give of our bodies. But may we begin looking for little ways to reconnect with our husbands despite the pain?

Sometimes it takes fighting through the agony and opening of ourselves to vulnerability, even in the midst of great turmoil. If this feels too difficult or painful, ask your husband for time to pray and seek the Lord. Take a preset amount of time to do so, but then return to your husband and fulfill your promise to meet him where his needs are. Blessing him in this way will also be a blessing to you, although at first, it may be very challenging. Keep asking and seeking for Jesus to meet you in that place and to give you a capacity to enjoy your husband again. Remember, He has already promised that He would!

For more on this topic, please read Robyn McKelvy's *SOS: Sick of Sex*. She has done such a beautiful job of putting together a comprehensive look at this very delicate subject.

At the beginning of this week, we stood at the bottom of our hill looking at the path upward. It has been a bit of a rocky climb for me, especially dealing with the difficult subjects of our sexual expression and finances. I'm guessing it has been challenging for you as well. However, I pray that it has been as much of a blessing to you as it has been for me. I hope that you have been able to have some good conversations with your husband and healing times of prayer throughout the week. I pray that you have been able to find some time alone to rediscover yourself and to plan for future successes. I know that regardless of the struggles you've dealt with this week, the very fact that you are sitting with me now means that you have journeyed forward. Even if it feels like we're taking two steps forward and one step back, it's still forward progression, isn't it?

I am greatly encouraged that we are half way done. Look back over the past three weeks, girl, and see how far we've traveled.

Come with me, dear one, let's continue onward and upward.

O fear the Lord, you His saints; For to those who fear Him there is no want. The young lions do lack and suffer hunger; But they who seek the Lord shall not be in want of any good thing.

(Psalm 34:9-10)

Week 4

KEEP YOUR TONGUE FROM EVIL
PSALM 34:11–14

Last week seemed to be very practical, down to the nitty-gritty, and externally focused. We looked at implementing ways to make life on the outside of ourselves a bit more bearable. We spent a lot of time on how to regain our own identities and seeking to have our needs and desires met in a non-self-serving manner.

This week, we are going to return to the more spiritual aspects of our healing while maintaining the practicality of purposefully working out our faith. We will look more at how to minister to our husbands while pursuing peace and lasting forgiveness. There is still much that we must work through, learn to trust Jesus for, and work out in practical application of our daily journeys.

I hope you are continuing to pray each day, asking your Redeemer to reveal the deep hidden recesses of your heart and teach you to apply to them the truths of His Word. I pray that you will continue seeking to keep an open mind and heart as we trek on through dark and sorrowful valleys, climb the rocky challenging cliffs of self-denial, and trudge through the muddy marshes of absolution.

DAY 1: THE FEAR OF THE LORD

But to man He said, "Behold, the reverential and worshipful fear of the Lord—that is wisdom; And to depart from evil is understanding." (Job 28:28 AMP)

Psalm 34:11–14 charges us,

> *Come, you children, listen to me; I will teach you the fear of the Lord. Who is the man who desires life And loves length of days that he may see good? Keep your tongue from evil And your lips from speaking deceit. Depart from evil and do good; Seek peace and pursue it.*

What else is there to say? Drop the mic and walk away, right? If we want to know the fear of the Lord, desire to lack *"no good thing,"* and want to be in a place of blessing (such that we have *"no want"*), it's all right in this little psalm. The instructions for how to practically live in God's presence and blessing are perfectly laid out in the midst of the praise and exhortation of this passage. We are to fear the Lord by keeping ourselves from evil, speaking truthfully, doing good, and pursuing peace.

Today we will focus mainly on the fear of the Lord and the meaning of truly honoring Him with our hearts. I believe keeping our tongue from evil is impossible unless we have committed ourselves to truly fearing God. As James says, "If anyone does not stumble in what he says, he is a perfect man, able to bridle the whole body as well … no one can tame the tongue; it is a restless evil and full of deadly poison" (James 3:2 and 8).

We have discussed some of these concepts already, but they are worth revisiting. The phrase "fear of the Lord" is used three times in the twenty-two verses of Psalm 34. Other similar phrases such as "seek Him," "take refuge in Him," and "the righteous" are used multiple times as well. The concept presented is that we must actively pursue an ongoing knowledge of and respect for our Creator.

There are two different Hebrew words used to express the concept of fearing the Lord. The first is *yare'*, which means "fearing; morally, reverent: afraid, fear."[29] The second word is *yir'ah*, which is translated "fear, terror, awesome, terrifying thing, respect, reverence."[30] Hebrews 10:31 says, "It is a terrifying thing to fall into the hands of the living God." The idea is that we ought to be in such awe and fear of God's power and holiness that we desire nothing more than to honor and obey Him. It's not that we fear judgement, for we know that we have been saved by the blood of Jesus, but out of deep reverence and respect for the perfect holiness of the Sovereign King, we rend our hearts and lives to worship Him.

An unhealthy fear, which is condemnation, is not our Redeemer's intention for us. As 1 John 4:18 points out, this type of fear is the opposite of love because it involves punishment or as the King James says "torment." However, a healthy fear of the Lord is necessary for the proper implementation of faith. We must believe that we are deserving of death and torment, and therefore, we approach the King with great reverence, honor, and gratitude. We take refuge in the fact that Jesus has paid the price for our wrongs and failures and look to Him to free us from our old ways of doing things, from regret, and the torment of unforgiveness.

Read Psalm 50:8–15.

1. What things does God consider as being righteous expressions of our reverence for Him?

_____

_____

_____

_____

Our King asks very little of us. He is not impressed with our sacrifices. The blood of bulls and rams does not appease His holy standard. He has no need of the things that we think we can offer Him because He already owns the whole world and everything in it. Our houses are His, our children are His, and the very breath in our lungs belongs to Him.

David says in Psalm 50 that we are to offer sacrifices of praise, keep our vows before the Lord (one of which is our marriage vow), and call upon Him in times of trouble. Reverencing our Creator means that we praise Him for all that He is and all that He has done. We exhaust all of our strength and resources to remain faithful to the promises that we have made to Him, both externally and internally (in the deep recesses of our hearts).

However, we are not to do it on our own. We offer these sacrifices by the power of *His* grace when we call upon *Him* for help. He expects that we will not attempt to serve or honor Him in our own strength, but rather, He commands us, "Call upon Me in the day of trouble" so that He may "rescue you, and you will honor [Him]" (Psalm 50:15).

2. Look at Romans 12:1–2 and identify another way in which we are to honor the Lord.

_____

_____

_____

_____

Paul urges us, "by the mercies of God, to present your bodies [dedicating all of yourselves, set apart] as a living sacrifice, holy and well-pleasing to God, which is your rational (logical, intelligent) act of worship" (AMP). He says yet again, that we do this not by our own power but by the mercies of God. We must acknowledge that because of what Jesus has done for us and all that the Father sacrificed in sending His Son, our "reasonable" and "logical" service is simply to offer ourselves fully and completely to Him. However, we can only do this by His mercy. In *My Utmost for His Highest*, Oswald Chambers says,

> If He is not the One to whom I am looking for direction and guidance, then there is no benefit in my sacrifice. But when my sacrifice is made with my eyes focused on Him, slowly but surely His molding influence becomes evident in my life.[31]

This means that sacrificing by remaining in our marriages in order to simply fulfill our vows isn't of any benefit to us. When six, ten, or twenty years later, we are still bitter and resentful and cry out to the Lord, saying, *Why haven't you fixed this? Why didn't you accept my sacrifice?* He will say to us as He said to Cain before he killed Abel,

> *Why are you so angry? And why do you look annoyed? If you do well [believing Me and doing what is acceptable and pleasing to Me], will you not be accepted? And if you do not do well [but ignore My instruction], sin crouches at your door; its desire is for you [to overpower you], but you must master it. (Genesis 4:6–7 AMP).*

Read the story of Cain and Abel in Genesis 4:2–8.

3. Examine Hebrews 11:4 and write the reason that Abel's sacrifice was pleasing to God but Cain's was not.

_____

_____

_____

_____

Remember how I said that all the reasons for staying in your marriage other than for the purpose of obeying the Lord would fail you? Staying for the sake of your parents, children, your pride, or even because it's the "right thing to do" will fail you. You must stay in order to honor the Lord. It must be done in faith as Abel's sacrifice was given.

The Lord said to Cain, "If you do well, will you not be accepted?" (Genesis 4:7). The Amplified Bible expounds upon what it means to do well. It says, "believing Me." Cain was not accepted because as Hebrews points out, something was not right in his heart. He was not acting in faith. Although he offered a sacrifice from his own labor and possibly even the firstfruits of his bounty, it wasn't about the type of offering, but it was about what was in his heart.

We too must look to Jesus to empower us to keep our vows. We must ask Him to be the reason for and the source of our ability to continue forward. He must be the One to whom we look for the ability to forgive and be restored on the inside. He is the One to whom we run when we are hurting and angry. We cast all our cares upon Him.

If we stay in our marriages as a form of sacrifice but do not do it by faith in the only One who can truly heal us, we sacrifice in vain. We will end up resentful and bitter. Our children and husbands, as well as our own souls, will suffer immensely. Truly fearing the Lord is walking with Him by faith, believing all He has done for us, and trusting all that He says.

Continuing in the study of sacrifices that are pleasing to the Lord, which is one way of expressing our fear of Him, let's examine another passage in Hebrews.

4. Read Hebrews 13:15–16 and write down what you learn.

_____

_____

_____

_____

5. Study Psalm 4:4–5. What sacrifices are we to offer to the Lord?

_____

_____

_____

_____

The most important form of fearing the Lord or of a sacrifice offered to Him may be the one spoken of by David in Psalm 51:15–17.

6. List the three sacrifices that David said are pleasing to God and the two that are not.

_____

_____

_____

_____

7. What does this passage say specifically to you?

_____

_____

_____

_____

I love the Amplified Bible's version of this text. Let's read it.

> *O Lord, open my lips, For You do not delight in sacrifice, or else I would give it; You are not pleased with burnt offering. My [only] sacrifice [acceptable] to God is a broken spirit; A broken and contrite heart [broken with sorrow for sin, thoroughly penitent], such, O God, You will not despise.*

Isn't it fascinating that David asked the Lord to open his lips? He again reminds us in Psalm 51 that it is only by the life and breath of the Holy Spirit dwelling within us that we are even capable of uttering praise.

David prayed this after his affair with Bathsheba had been made known to Nathan the prophet. His sin had found him out, as Numbers 32:23 puts it, and David was before the Lord repenting. He recognized with deep reverence and a sorrowful spirit that he could not make the wrongs he had done right.

Previously, in Psalm 51:4, he said, "Against You, You only, I have sinned And done what is evil in Your sight," recognizing that it was against God's holiness that he had done this evil thing. David acknowledged that there was no sacrifice great enough to cover his sin and that he was left only at the mercy of the Lord. All David had to offer as reparation was praise, a broken spirit, and a contrite heart. Yet those were the very things that God did not despise. This is the place where we are to begin and end our pursuit of the fear of the Lord.

8. Read Mark 12:28–34. Explain what the scribe says is more important than all our offerings and sacrifices.

_____

_____

_____

_____

9. Does Jesus agree with his assertion? _____

10. Is the scribe's statement in agreement with what David said in Psalm 51?

☐   Yes

☐   No

11. Read Psalm 51:16–19 in the New Living Translation of the Bible and put your name in the blanks.

> _You do not desire a sacrifice, or I would offer one. You do not want a burnt offering. The sacrifice you desire is a broken spirit. You will not reject _____'s broken and repentant heart, O God._
> _Look with favor on _____ and help her; rebuild the walls of _____'s [home and life]._
> _Then you will be pleased with [my] sacrifices offered in the right spirit— with burnt offerings and whole burnt offerings. Then [the motives of my heart] will again be sacrificed on your altar._

12. Based on what you have read today, write in your own words what the Bible says we ought to do in order to display our fear of the Lord.

_____

_____

_____

_____

13. What are some ways that you can begin to put these principles into practice?

_____

_____

_____

_____

DAY 2: THE POWER OF THE TONGUE

There is one who speaks rashly like the thrusts of a sword, But
the tongue of the wise brings healing. (Proverbs 12:18)

As I prepare for each lesson, it seems that the Lord also prepares me by first taking me down the road on which we are about to embark. I have walked into several ditches and traversed a few muddy gullies in the course of writing these studies. I am often humbled at my failings and inconsistencies and reminded of the immeasurable grace of my Redeemer in allowing me the honor of putting these words on paper. I can only hope and pray that it is for His glory and your good—it is definitely for *my* good.

This lesson is one such journey in which I've been humbled yet again. Not even realizing that we would be discussing the power of the tongue, I was convicted multiple times this past week about my speech and the attitude in which I opened my mouth. So it is with a humble heart that I begin today's journey. Please know that this is equally convicting for me, as it hopefully will be for you.

At times, it is excruciating to have the Holy Spirit bring to my recollection the things that I have said in certain circumstances, revealing to me how displeased or dishonored He was in them. Yet I am so very grateful that He continues to pursue me and open my eyes to the things that He is still working out in me. God has not left me as I am nor as I was, but He patiently continues to reveal the actions or attitudes that require repentance and my surrender to Him.

I pray that you are also learning to be grateful for the Holy Spirit's conviction in your heart. I pray that we may be faithful to tell Him each day, "Search me, O God, and know my heart; Try me, and know my anxieties; And see if there is any wicked way in me, And lead me in the way everlasting" (Psalm 139:23–24 NKJV). If you haven't been praying this prayer, let today begin a new purposefulness in your heart, as we dive into the study of our words.

1. Read Matthew 12:33–37 and underline all of Jesus's assertions about our speech.

> *Either make the tree good and its fruit good, or else make the tree bad*
> *and its fruit bad; for a tree is known by its fruit. Brood of vipers! How*
> *can you, being evil, speak good things? For out of the abundance of the*
> *heart the mouth speaks. A good man out of the good treasure of his heart*

brings forth good things, and an evil man out of the evil treasure brings forth evil things. But I say to you that for every idle word men may speak, they will give account of it in the day of judgment. For by your words you will be justified, and by your words you will be condemned. (NKJV)

2. Explain in your own words what Jesus is teaching us about the use of our speech.

_____

_____

_____

_____

Flip over to James 1:12–27. Pay careful attention to the whole concept. Our Bibles often break things up into sections for easy reading, but that was not the intent of the writers. Much of what is spoken is designed to build upon itself.

James 1:14 says, "Each one is tempted when [she] is carried away and enticed by [her] own lust." The New King James Version says, "When [she] is drawn away by [her] own desires and enticed." Oswald Chambers defines spiritual lust as, "I must have it at once."[32] Oh, how often we are carried away by ugly words because we have become angry that our lusts have not been fulfilled.

Have you ever wanted your husband to say or do something to make you feel better in the midst of a difficulty, to encourage you, or meet your need for security when it has been damaged, but he failed miserably? Have you then gotten angry, said hurtful words, and thrown his wrongs back in his face? I have. Have you ever said, "If you really knew me," or, "If you really loved me," or the one I'm most ashamed of, "If you were truly sorry [for his indiscretions]"? These are the dragging away of our own spiritual lusts. Ouch, right? I am sorry to say that I have used these and many other damaging words to try to manipulate and shame my husband into acting or not acting in a certain manner. Have you done this?

3. What desires or lusts do you find yourself getting angry over when they are not met or fulfilled?

_____

_____

_____

_____

4. What hateful words have you said or been tempted to say in those circumstances?

_____

_____

_____

_____

5. Read James 1:15 again. What does sin give birth to? _____

6. What does it mean for your marriage when you use hurtful language toward your spouse?

_____

_____

_____

_____

Our spiritual lusts can drag us away into hateful speech and damaging attitudes toward our husbands, which produce death in our hearts, their hearts, and ultimately, the marriage itself.

However, James offers us an alternative. James 1:16–18 tells us that our Father offers us good and perfect gifts in exchange for our submission to His desires for us. We don't have to be dragged off into death. Rather, we can look to Him to make us the firstfruits of His creation, or as the Amplified Bible puts it, "a prime example of what He created to be set apart to Himself—sanctified, made holy for His divine purposes" (James 1:18). We are given the opportunity to live by His word of truth rather than being controlled by our impulses.

7. Look again at verses 19–20 and fill in the blanks.

"Know this, my beloved brothers: let every person be quick to hear, slow to _____, slow to _____; for the anger of man does not produce the _____ of God" (ESV).

What more can be said? I think we all know exactly what this means for own our lives. It means that already today, we have failed, and we will fail at least five more times before the day is out. Am I right? It means that we desperately need a Savior. It means that we need to ask the Holy Spirit to work continually and effectually in us to accomplish all that we are unable to accomplish on our own.

I want to focus on one little statement. Look at the last phrase again, "the anger of man does not produce the righteousness of God" (James 1:20). Remember what we learned about trying to manipulate or force our husbands into behaving or speaking in certain ways to fulfill our spiritual lusts? Isn't it interesting that God addresses that idea directly in this verse? Though it seems to mean that our anger doesn't produce the righteousness within us that God requires, I believe we can also take it to mean that we can never force the righteousness of God into someone else's life by our use of angry words.

Man, this one stings a lot when I think of the way that I speak to my children. My frustrated tone and the repetitive teaching (i.e. lecturing) in which I attempt to cram some lesson into their heads will never accomplish God's righteousness in their hearts. This only comes by the power of the Holy Spirit working in their lives and His grace. The same is true of our husbands, coworkers, friends, and unbelieving family members.

Instead of angry words and hurtful tones, we are told to "put away all filthiness and rampant wickedness and receive with meekness the implanted word, which is able to save your souls" (James 1:21 ESV). With humility, which is translated here as *meekness*, we are to receive the Word of God—the same Word that says we must put away filthy speech, angry, hurtful words, incessant nagging, and rampant wickedness.

Read James1:22–27 again in the Amplified Bible.

But prove yourselves doers of the word [actively and continually obeying God's precepts], and not merely listeners [who hear the word but fail to internalize its meaning], deluding yourselves [by unsound reasoning contrary to the truth]. For if anyone only listens to the word without obeying it, he is like a man who looks very carefully at his natural face in a mirror; for once he has looked at himself and gone away, he immediately forgets what he looked like. But he who looks carefully into the perfect law, the law of liberty, and faithfully abides by it, not having become a [careless] listener who forgets but an active doer [who obeys], he will be blessed and favored by God in what he does [in his life of obedience]. If anyone thinks himself to be religious [scrupulously observant of the rituals of his faith], and does not control his tongue but deludes his own heart, this person's religion is worthless (futile, barren). Pure and unblemished religion [as it is expressed in outward acts] in the sight of our God and Father is this: to visit and look after the fatherless and the widows in their distress, and to keep oneself uncontaminated by the [secular] world.

The Word of God is to be like a mirror where we can see ourselves the way that our Redeemer desires us to be. If we simply read the words (look into the mirror) and walk away unchanged, we will never become all that He means for us to be. We must accept His words and ask for His provision (empowering, grace, and ability) to change us into the image of Himself.

Then by faith, we must obey what we have read. We must let the conviction about the way language should be spoken within our homes do more than just move us to sorrow. We must act on that sorrow to implement change. We replace hateful speech with words of gentleness, "gracious and pleasant, seasoned with salt … [at] all times," as Colossians 4:6 tells us (AMP).

Remember that salt makes things taste better, causes you to want to go back for more (bet you can't eat just one potato chip!), and makes you thirsty. Of course, the thirst should be other people's desire to have more of Jesus, who is the Living Water, after having been in our presence. They should receive even our rebukes with graciousness and gratitude because of the pleasant way that we present it. Proverbs tells us, "Pleasant words are a honeycomb, Sweet to the soul and healing to the bones" (Proverbs 16:24), and "Faithful are the wounds of a friend" (Proverbs 27:6).

8. What are some ways you can begin to replace hurtful language with words that are "seasoned with salt?"

_____

_____

_____

_____

Peter tells us that we must also replace our worthless religion and the poor use of our tongues with words that honor the Lord. True religion that is honoring to Jesus is loving and caring for orphans and widows as He did. Imagine how much easier it will be to speak graciously to our children when we realize how terrible the lives of orphans can be. How much easier it is to appreciate our husbands when we consider the lives of those who have lost their spouses?

Something happens in our hearts when we begin to care for others who are in more difficult circumstances than our own. We learn to appreciate the life we have, and gratitude fills our hearts as we see the challenges in the lives of others. Not only that, but we prove our love for Jesus by our love and care for those whom He loves and cares for. He said in Matthew 25:40, "Whatever you did for one of the least of these brothers and sisters of mine, you did for me" (NIV).

James continues his discourse on the tongue (as if we're not cut to the heart enough yet) in chapter 3.

9. Read James 3:1–12 and express your response to the Holy Spirit.

_____

_____

_____

_____

10. Look up Deuteronomy 30:19 and write the choice given to you by God today.

I have the choice between _____ and _____, between _____ and _____.

As we have already said, our words can bring life or death, but we've just seen that they can also bring blessing or cursing. We have the choice to speak life and blessing over our husbands and our marriages or death and cursing. Lord Jesus, help us to choose life!

Ephesians 4:25–32 gives us some very practical examples of what proper speech is and isn't supposed to sound like. Let's read it in the Amplified Bible to gain a broader understanding of how to use our language for blessing rather than harm.

> *Therefore, rejecting all falsehood [whether lying, defrauding, telling half-truths, spreading rumors, any such as these], speak truth each one with his neighbor, for we are all parts of one another [and we are all parts of the body of Christ]. Be angry [at sin—at immorality, at injustice, at ungodly behavior], yet do not sin; do not let your anger [cause you shame, nor allow it to] last until the sun goes down. And do not give the devil an opportunity [to lead you into sin by holding a grudge, or nurturing anger, or harboring resentment, or cultivating bitterness]. The thief [who has become a believer] must no longer steal, but instead he must work hard [making an honest living], producing that which is good with his own hands, so that he will have something to share with those in need. Do not let unwholesome [foul, profane, worthless, vulgar] words ever come out of your mouth, but only such speech as is good for building up others, according to the need and the occasion, so that it will be a blessing to those who hear [you speak]. And do not grieve the Holy Spirit of God [but seek to please Him], by whom you were sealed and marked [branded as God's own] for the day of redemption [the final deliverance from the consequences of sin]. Let all bitterness and wrath and anger and clamor [perpetual animosity, resentment, strife, fault-finding] and slander be put away from you, along with every kind of malice [all spitefulness, verbal abuse, malevolence]. Be kind and helpful to one another, tender-hearted [compassionate, understanding], forgiving one another [readily and freely], just as God in Christ also forgave you.*

11. According to this passage, discuss if is it wrong to be angry.

_____

_____

_____

_____

12. Whom do we most offend by our careless words?

_____

_____

_____

I have often heard it taught that if you want to be successful in long-term change, you must replace negative behaviors with positive ones. We don't just quit snacking because we want to give up potato chips, but we replace them with carrots, sunflower seeds, or apples, right? The same is true of our spiritual diet. It wouldn't really work to just stop one action. It must be replaced with a better, more purposeful action.

13. Ephesians 4 tells us to replace sinful habits with new attitudes and behaviors. List them below.

_____

_____

_____

_____

We have the freedom, by the power Jesus's blood, to call out to the Holy Spirit and ask Him to give us the ability to replace lying, exaggeration, and manipulative and bitter language with kind words, helpfulness, tenderhearted compassion, and forgiveness.

14. Write a prayer of repentance regarding your speech and ask the Holy Spirit to replace those things with new life-giving words of blessing.

_____

_____

_____

_____

DAY 3: LOVE WITHOUT HYPOCRISY

Therefore humble yourselves under the mighty hand of God,
that He may exalt you at the proper time. (1 Peter 5:6)

Father,

In humility, we come to You today, recognizing that we are so unworthy, so faithless, so unfaithful, and in desperate need of Your healing, mercy, and grace. Please forgive us for all the wretchedness that we carry in our hearts and the pet sins that we harbor. Please take from us the evil pride of life, to which we cling so tightly, and teach us instead, to pursue humility. By Your power and in the name of Your Son, Jesus, amen.

After the rough day that we had yesterday, I feel like we need to take a deep breath, grab a cup of tea, and put up our feet for a bit. But we don't have time for that, my friend. We must continue climbing. This one is going to be rocky for us too, but let's keep at it with diligence. We want to be transformed, don't we?

The *Merriam-Webster Dictionary* defines *hypocrisy* as, "A feigning to be what one is not or to believe what one does not: behavior that contradicts what one claims to believe or feel … the false assumption of an appearance of virtue or religion."[33]

Wow! That one hurts, doesn't it? How often do you and I feign to believe what we do not believe or to be what we are not, especially when it comes to our love for others? We claim to be loving and kind, but we often act in direct contradiction to those claims. We learned yesterday that we use of our tongues to claim, "I love you," one minute but the next minute, turn around to spew out words laced with venom. We claim to have forgiven our husbands but then act in a way that's completely contradictory to forgiveness. True love, as defined by the Bible, is free of hypocrisy. We are called to love with meekness, gentleness, and Christ-like authenticity.

Today, we are going to focus on Romans 12 and study what our King wants for us when He calls us to love without hypocrisy. Read Romans 12:9–21 in your own translation. Then read it in the New American Standard Bible version below.

Let love be without hypocrisy. Abhor what is evil; cling to what is good. Be devoted to one another in brotherly love; give preference to one another in honor; not lagging behind in diligence, fervent in spirit, serving the Lord; rejoicing in hope, persevering in tribulation, devoted to prayer, contributing to the needs of the saints, practicing hospitality. Bless those who persecute you; bless and do not curse. Rejoice with those who rejoice, and weep with those who weep. Be of the same mind toward one another; do not be haughty in mind, but associate with the lowly. Do not be wise in your own estimation. Never pay back evil for evil to anyone. Respect what is right in the sight of all men. If possible, so far as it depends on you, be at peace with all men. Never take your own revenge, beloved, but leave room for the wrath of God, for it is written, "Vengeance is Mine, I will repay," says the Lord. "But if your enemy is hungry, feed him, and if he is thirsty, give him a drink; for in so doing you will heap burning coals on his head." Do not be overcome by evil, but overcome evil with good.

1. Count all the evil things that we are told to avoid or to stop doing.

How many did you find? _____

2. List the good things that we are told to do to replace our bad behaviors.

_____	_____
_____	_____
_____	_____
_____	_____
_____	_____
_____	_____
_____	_____
_____	_____
_____	_____

Wow! There were five negative commands and twenty-four replacement behaviors. That's enough to keep us busy for an entire lifetime.

3. Which commands were the most convicting to you, and why was this so?

_____

_____

_____

_____

When we consider love without hypocrisy, we must examine all that love entails: what it is and what it is not. Love is not arrogant, boastful, self-seeking, or easily provoked. It does not keep a record of wrongs. It is not rude or jealous (see 1 Corinthians 13:4–8). Love does not continue to bring up the past, which is simply stated as unforgiveness. It does not throw little sharp daggers or sideways insults, excuse its poor behavior, or think it is a lesser sinner than others. It is not easily drawn into fits of anger. It is not jealous of coworkers, classmates, fellow church members, children, spouses, or others' gifts, talents, freedoms, accomplishments, or friendships.

When we explore what love is, we learn that love is gracious, patient, and kind. It "bears all things, believes all things, hopes all things, endures all things" (1 Corinthians 13:7). Love believes that her spouse is not the enemy and hopes for his complete repentance and God's healing. Love endures the heartaches that come with life and relationships and bears the burden of walking this thing out until healing has come and restoration is complete.

"Love never fails" (1 Corinthians 13:8). Love *never* fails. My friend, if we are pleading with the Holy Spirit to fill our hearts with the love of Jesus, *we cannot fail*. Do you believe that? His love never fails. His love *in* us will not fail.

We have learned in the past that we shouldn't allow repetitious sin, falsehood, or abuse to remain unchecked in our marriages. I want to remind us of this again briefly, but from a different direction. Notice with me what 1 Corinthians 13:6 says love does not do. "[Love] does not rejoice in unrighteousness, but rejoices with the truth." We must be careful not to condone lying, cheating, or unrighteous behavior while maintaining no record of wrongs. Love does not permit someone to continue in persistent sin. This is tricky because we are not called to be the Holy Spirit in the lives of others, but if our husbands maintain certain sinful behaviors, we are permitted by scripture and required by love to confront them.

4. Read and rewrite Matthew 18:15–16 in your own words.

_____

_____

_____

_____

We are instructed by Jesus to go to our brother (in this case our husband) and to "tell him his fault, between you and him alone" (Matthew 18:15 ESV), or as other translations say, "In private." We don't drag out their faults or failures or belittle them in front of our children or other church members. We don't bad-mouth them to our friends (Ouch, right? That one got me in trouble this week). We simply go to them in private and address our concerns.

Jesus does not permit us to nag or nitpick. Proverbs says, "A nagging wife is like the dripping of a leaky roof in a rainstorm. Stopping her is like trying to stop the wind" (Proverbs 27:15-16 NIRV). Rather, we pray for our husbands, seek the will of the Lord in our circumstances, perhaps seek godly counsel, and then lovingly address the sin.

As Jesus said in verse 16, if our husbands are unresponsive, we may need to take a couple of people with us or seek a pastor or marriage counselor to help encourage our husbands to properly deal with their sins. If you have not requested that your husband join you in counseling with a pastor, biblical counselor, or church elder, please, please do so.

Perhaps, we are not to address our husbands' sins at all, but we are called to simply begin silently praying that the Holy Spirit would convict them. Again, this depends upon the severity of the sin. Certainly, continual accessing of pornography or inappropriate behavior toward other women are not excusable, however, lying or cheating at work may not necessarily be our issue to address. Excessive or frivolous spending may be a gray area where we have to pray and ask the Spirit to give us direction as to whether or not to bring it to our husbands' attention.

Of course, we don't want to be silent while our husbands spend our families' money until we are bankrupt. Perhaps for certain expenses, we need to pray that they see how irresponsible they are being or allow them to experience the consequences of their own behaviors (or attitudes), even if that means a bit of suffering or sacrifice for us. First Peter says,

When they hurled their insults at him, he did not retaliate; when he suffered, he made no threats. Instead, he entrusted himself to him who judges justly. "He himself bore our sins" in his body on the cross, so that we might die to sins and live for righteousness; "by his wounds you have been healed." For "you were like sheep going astray," but now you have returned to the Shepherd and Overseer of your souls ... Wives, in the same way submit yourselves to your own husbands so that, if any of them do not believe the word, they may be won over without words by the behavior of their wives, when they see the purity and reverence of your lives. (1 Peter 2:23–3:2, NIV)

Determining which response is appropriate for our husbands' behaviors requires a great deal of discernment. Obviously, if our husbands ask us to participate in something that we believe is wrong, we are protected by scripture when we "obey God rather than men" (Acts 5:29). There is a fine line between being permissive and enabling and being gracious and allowing the Holy Spirit to do His work. Much prayer is required here.

Please, also keep in mind that we are to address the sin in these circumstances and not our husbands' personhood or characters. Remember, we are told to love the person but hate the sin.

5. Read Psalm 119:161–166. What and whom do the writer hate?

_____

_____

_____

_____

6. In Matthew 5:43–48, what does Jesus say that we are to do to and for those who curse, hate, or spitefully use us (NKJV)?

_____

_____

_____

_____

7. This makes our love _____ as our Heavenly Father's love is _____.

Consider what the apostle John says in 1 John 2:3–11, with regard to love and hate.

8. How have you been walking in the light with regard to love?

_____

_____

_____

_____

9. How have you been walking in darkness?

_____

_____

_____

_____

> "So put aside every trace of malice and all deceit and hypocrisy and envy and all slander and hateful speech; like newborn babies (you should) long for the pure milk of the word, so that by it you may be nurtured and grow in respect to salvation (its ultimate fulfillment), if in fact you have (already) tasted the goodness and gracious kindness of the Lord."
>
> (1 Peter 2:1–3, AMP)

Love is completely self-sacrificing. It's willing to risk itself and risk being mistreated in order to pursue perfect union with another. Jesus's love was so perfect toward us that He willing took our punishment and carried our sorrows. He was abused and spat upon. He was beaten and cursed. Surely, we are not suffering to that extent under our husbands' sinful or fleshly decisions. Let's begin seeking to display sincere love to our husbands.

10. In what ways have you been hypocritical with your love?

_____

_____

_____

_____

11. Ask the Holy Spirit to make your love toward your husband sincere and without hypocrisy.

_____

_____

_____

_____

DAY 4: GLORY AND PRAISE

I cried to him with my mouth, and high praise was on my tongue. (Psalm 66:17)

A few times, we have discussed how important is it to replace bad behaviors with good or positive ones. At church this past Sunday, the pastor said that you don't just clear a field of the weeds and then leave it empty because in no time, it will be filled with weeds again.[34] Instead of leaving the field empty, you plant something in place of the weeds. Then the ground and the water become useful rather than remaining barren.

Today we will focus on the things that we can say, think, or pray to replace our ugly speech, harmful thoughts, and careless words. The most effective way that I have found to pull the weeds of careless speech is to plant seeds of praise in my heart. When we are praising our King, worshiping Him for who He is and what He has done, we are less inclined to be hurtful toward others. When we are glorifying our Redeemer for all that He has rescued us from, we are less likely to be overly critical of those around us. We are unable to use our tongues for evil when they are busy with songs of joy and blessing.

Additionally, if we are speaking blessing and praise over others, our heart attitude toward them automatically begins to shift. When we are intentional about speaking blessing over others, our love for them blossoms, our minds begin to believe, on a much deeper level, the things we have spoken, and our attitudes toward them change.

1. Recall what we learned yesterday in Romans 12:14 about our speech toward others. Write it below.

_____

_____

_____

_____

Paul encourages us to bless others and not curse them. Sometimes, we find this exceptionally difficult when others treat us poorly or we have been deeply wounded, particularly by our own husbands. However, the more ways that we can find to speak honor to them, the more we begin to appreciate them and view them with the eyes of their Redeemer, rather than through our own wounded-ness. Let's continue to look at what Jesus has to say about the words we speak.

2. Read the following proverbs and highlight (or underline) the wisdom we are given regarding what comes out of our mouths.

Proverbs 10:18–20

> *Whoever conceals hatred with lying lips and spreads slander is a fool. Sin is not ended by multiplying words, but the prudent hold their tongues. The tongue of the righteous is choice silver, but the heart of the wicked is of little value. The lips of the righteous nourish many, but fools die for lack of sense.* (NIV)

Proverbs 11:9, 11

> *The hypocrite with [her] mouth destroys [her] neighbor, But through knowledge the righteous will be delivered … By the blessing of the upright the city is exalted, But it is overthrown by the mouth of the wicked* (NKJV).

Proverbs 11:12–13

> *[She] who despises [her] neighbor lacks sense, But a [woman] of understanding keeps silent. [She] who goes about as a talebearer reveals secrets, But [she] who is trustworthy conceals a matter.*

Proverbs 11:22

> *A beautiful woman who lacks discretion is like a gold ring in a pig's snout.*

Proverbs 12:4

> *An excellent wife is the crown of her husband, But she who shames him is like rottenness in his bones.*

Proverbs 12:16

A fool's anger is known at once, But a prudent [woman] conceals dishonor.

Proverbs 12:22–23, 25

Lying lips are an abomination to the Lord, But those who deal faithfully are His delight. A prudent [woman] conceals knowledge, But the heart of fools proclaims folly ... Anxiety in a man's heart weighs it down, But a good word makes it glad.

Proverbs 31:10, 26

An excellent wife, who can find? For her worth is far above jewels ... She opens her mouth in wisdom, And the teaching of kindness is on her tongue.

3. Write three key phrases that stuck out to you in these verses and explain how they relate to your current circumstances.

Key Phrase 1

_____

_____

_____

_____

Key Phrase 2

_____

_____

_____

_____

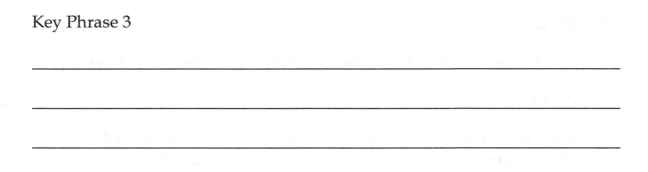

Proverbs is full of wisdom regarding our speech as well as how we are to handle our attitudes toward others. Not only are we admonished to hold our tongues in times of anger or hurt but also are instructed to use our words to encourage and build up those around us. This is true especially of our husbands, to whom you and I were given as gifts.

"House and wealth are an inheritance from fathers, But a prudent wife is from the Lord" (Proverbs 19:14). Did you catch that? You and I are given by the Lord to our husbands because He said it is not good for men to be alone (Genesis 2:18). This isn't because we put up with so much from them or we are on this earth simply to make their dinner and pick up their dirty underwear. We are their *ezer*, their helper and encourager, remember?

When we speak blessing, gratitude, and encouragement over them, it's like the refreshment of biting into a cold, sweet apple. Our words are as valuable as gold in their eyes. King Solomon says, "Like apples of gold in settings of silver Is a word spoken at the right time" (Proverbs 25:11 AMP). Sometimes we are the only source of encouragement our husbands receive throughout the day. Conversely, we may be the only source of discouragement and scorn.

My hope is that we will begin to breathe life into our men by reminding them that we appreciate them, even in the smallest of things. We can say, "Hey, thanks for taking out the trash," "I really appreciated you playing with the kids so I could read a book," or, "Thank you for going to work today to provide for our family." We can encourage them by letting them know that they are worth the energy and effort that it takes to heal our marriages. We can remind them that we are grateful for their repentance and willingness to work it out alongside us.

It is important to look for little things to praise the men in our lives for. They don't necessarily show it, but they are in desperate need of our approval and encouragement. However, I know that as with many of the things we have discussed along this journey, finding ways to speak blessing into the lives of our husbands may be the last thing that we want to do or even feel capable of doing. I know that at times, it is exceptionally hard to find things to thank them for when it seems that they are the source of our pain and sorrow.

Please remember these two things, my dear friend: your husband is not the enemy (source of your sorrow). Sin, the world, and Satan are the enemies. Secondly, we are *not alone*. Jesus has not left us to fight alone or wrestle this out on our own. We have help and power in His presence. Read 2 Corinthians 1:21 in the translations below, linger for a while on who is doing the work in us, and consider what might be His purpose.

> *Now it is God who establishes and confirms us [in joint fellowship] with you in Christ, and who has anointed us [empowering us with the gifts of the Spirit].* (AMP)

> *It is God who enables us, along with you, to stand firm for Christ. He has commissioned us.* (NLT)

> *Now it is God who makes both us and you stand firm in Christ. He anointed us.* (NIV)

4. What did you notice as you meditated on this verse?

_____

_____

_____

_____

The Holy Spirit, who is within us, enables, empowers, and establishes us to stand firm in Jesus and to do the work that He has commanded us to do. Loving without hypocrisy, speaking blessing rather than cursing, and finding ways to praise and honor our husbands, are all done by the His Spirit's power at work in us.

5. Take a look at Zechariah 4:6 and write down what you discover.

_____

_____

_____

_____

I love the New Living Translation's rendering of this verse. It says, "It is not by force nor by strength, but by my Spirit, says the Lord of Heaven's Armies." It is not by force. We don't have to force ourselves to find things to praise our husbands for. We simply have to *ask Jesus* to make them a reality in our minds and hearts.

Spend a few minutes in prayer now. Ask Jesus, your King, to show you some things that you can praise your husband for this week. Ask the Holy Spirit to give you a thankful heart toward him.

6. Write down what He shows you and then tell a few of them to your husband.

_____

_____

_____

_____

As we consider our lives regarding loving and serving our King, we ought to be mindful that the work we serve Him in is not our own. Remember that 2 Corinthians 1:21 shows us it is *His* work, for *His* purposes, and for *His glory*. When we embrace this fact, we can't help but praise Him. We look at all He has accomplished in our hearts, we see the restoration that He has brought to our relationships, and we can't help but worship. All our working is to be done because He has made us to do it so that we might be an example of His glory and cause the praise of others.

7. Look up the following passages and fill in the blanks below.

Matthew 5:16

> Let your light so shine before men, that they may _____
> your _____ works and _____ your
> Father in heaven.

2 Corinthians 9:13

> Because of the service by which you have proved yourselves,
> others will _____ God for the
> _____ that accompanies your confession of
> the gospel of Christ. (NIV)

1 Peter 2:12

> Keep your conduct among the [unbelievers] _____
> , so that when they speak against you as evildoers, they may see your
> _____ deeds and _____ God on the day
> of visitation. (ESV)

We are called, not only to praise our King but also to be the cause for others to praise Him when they observe our lives. What an incredible thought this is to consider: Our unbelieving family members will be drawn to praise the living God when they see our marriages thriving, even after such a massive blow. It will bring glory to our Redeemer when they see us choose not to speak poorly of our husbands but to pour *blessing* out over them.

Jesus is worthy of all our honor and praise for all He has done. We are at our best when we are glorifying Him. We've talked about replacing evil thoughts with good ones, hurtful words with blessings, and filling our hearts with gratitude toward our husbands so that we can replace anger with joy. The best way to accomplish all these things is to let our hearts and mouths be filled with gratitude and praise to our Savior. As we choose to worship Him irrespective of our feelings, our hearts can't help but begin to fill with joy and peace. In time, this joy will replace the sorrow and resentment.

We will finish today with words from Psalms. I pray that these passages will lift your spirits as much as they do mine.

8. Read the following verses and pray them back to Jesus, our Redeemer.

Psalm 51:15–17

_____

_____

_____

_____

Psalm 149:1–9 (Remember that the sword in our hand is the Word of God)

_____

_____

_____

_____

Psalm 50:1–6

_____

_____

_____

_____

Psalm 77:10–20

_____

_____

_____

_____

Psalm 89:1–9

_____

_____

_____

_____

Psalm 97:1–6

_____

_____

_____

_____

DAY 5: FORGIVENESS

*And forgive us our debts, as we have forgiven our debtors [letting go
of both the wrong and the resentment]. (Matthew 6:12 AMP)*

What an accomplishment it is to be finishing up another week. We have spent much of our time this week looking at all the ways our speech affects our marriages, our families, and all those around us. We have discussed replacing evil thoughts and words with those of gratitude and praise, but what if we are still struggling to forgive? It seems impossible to speak blessing over a man with whom we are still so angry, doesn't it? We want to scream and cry out, "It's not fair! How can I be expected to bless him when he has brought so much cursing on me?"

Today we are going to address how to practically implement real and lasting forgiveness into our language, thoughts, and attitudes so that our love will be without hypocrisy. Jesus didn't call us only to forgive the easily forgiven. He called us to forgive all "our debtors" just as we also have been forgiven (Matthew 6:12).

In order to truly understand what it means to offer forgiveness, we need to look at the *act* of forgiving and grasp how to accomplish it in our hearts and minds. According to the Greater Good Science Center at University of California, Berkeley, forgiveness is

> A conscious, deliberate decision to release feelings of resentment or vengeance toward a person or group who has harmed you, regardless of whether they actually deserve your forgiveness … [forgiveness] brings the forgiver peace of mind and frees him or her from corrosive anger … it empowers you to recognize the pain you suffered without letting that pain define you, enabling you to heal and move on with your life.[35]

The Bible scholars at Got Questions define forgiveness in this way,

> It has no connection to weakness or even to emotions. Instead, forgiveness is an act of the will. Forgiveness is not granted because a person deserves to be forgiven. No one deserves to be

forgiven. Forgiveness is a deliberate act of love, mercy, and grace. Forgiveness is a decision to not hold something against another person, despite what he or she has done to you.[36]

Did you get that? Forgiveness "has no connection … to emotions." It is not a feeling.[37] Forgiveness is a *choice*. It is "a conscious, deliberate decision to release" our emotions.[38] Both biblical scholars and worldly psychologists agree that we forgive by deliberate decision, not by having a feeling of forgiveness or pleasurable thoughts toward that person.

As we have discussed in previous lessons, sometimes forgiving requires us to constantly make the choice not to hold grievances against ourselves or others. This may mean that we must choose forgiveness repeatedly throughout our days or weeks as circumstances that remind us of our heartache arise. In the midst of an argument, we choose not to drag out old wrongs. When hurt by a related situation, we decide not to bring up the wound. When frustrated with our own failings, we remember that we are forgiven and made new by the blood of Jesus.

This requires prayer, decisiveness, and commitment, but it does not require feelings. As we pray and make conscious choices to *act* in forgiveness, the Holy Spirit will begin to bring about the feelings of grace, mercy, and compassion in our hearts.

I personally do not believe forgiveness is ever an emotion that we feel, which seems to be the stance of many authors and pastors. Although I continue to choose forgiveness toward my husband, there is no emotion associated with it in my heart. The emotions that accompany my forgiveness are compassion, empathy, love, and gratitude, but forgiveness itself remains a decision that is made by the conscious act of my *will*.

Before we begin searching out forgiveness in our hearts for our husbands, we first need to spend time pursing forgiveness for ourselves. Over the course of these weeks, we have been asking Jesus to forgive us for the various things that the His Spirit has convicted us of, as we've come across them in our studies. However, have we been able to internalize His forgiveness and apply it to forgiving ourselves? If you don't feel that you need to forgive yourself, come along on this journey with the rest of us and pray that we will see the truth of Christ's redemption.

I want to remind those of us who have battled blaming ourselves for our husbands' failings that although we may have said and done things that were not beneficial to our marriages or our men, you and I are not to blame for their choices. It's wise for you and me to be careful to love and respect our husbands well, to be their biggest fans, and the crown of glory that they wear with joy. However, we cannot be held responsible for the decisions that they have made in our absence. For some of us, I know that it is gut wrenching to think of all the ways we have failed to love, respect, and appreciate the men God has given us.

Personally, I battled with a lot of self-blame because I had been withholding myself, both emotionally and physically, from my husband. I was so wounded by the many years of strife that our marriage had suffered. Because we had seen so little of each other over the course of the previous couple of years, I had withdrawn from him. I still loved him and wanted desperately for him to draw me back to himself, but I kept him at an arm's distance and built walls around my heart.

I said some very hurtful things in my desperate cries for his attention. I hadn't intended to hurt him, but it was wrong for me to have said those things, nonetheless. It was wrong for me to expect him to be the one to save me from the heartaches that I was suffering. Only Jesus can save us from our heartaches. As a man in need of comfort and reassurance, he found no solace in my arms because my arms were full of my own issues. So he turned to the arms of another woman.

Although my husband pursued many faulty habits during that time and sought a lifestyle that was contrary to the Word of God and despite all my fervent prayers, I still felt a lot of guilt for my responsibility in what had happened. At a marriage conference I attended many years ago, one of the speakers said, "Even if only 10% of the problems in the marriage are your responsibility, you need to take care of your ten percent." I felt that I had failed at my 10 percent.

1. Do you feel that you've failed at your 10, 5, or even 2 percent? Why or why not?

_____

_____

_____

_____

Regardless of whether we had any responsibility in the wrongs that were done to us, we still sometimes suffer much guilt and shame. In order to truly be able to forgive ourselves, we need to renew our minds with the truth of Jesus's forgiveness. Let's remember what has been done for us so that we can have freedom from shame.

Read 2 Corinthians 5:21.

> *For God made Christ, who never sinned, to be the offering for our sin, so that we could be made right with God through Christ.*

2. According to 2 Corinthians 5:21, who *became* sin for us?

_____

_____

_____

_____

3. Read Romans 10:11. Who will not be shamed?

_____

_____

_____

_____

4. Do you believe on Him?

□ Yes

□ No

If you answered yes, complete the verse with your name:

For the Scripture says, "_____, *who believes on Him will not be put to shame.*"

Isaiah 61:7 says, "*Instead of shame and dishonor, you will enjoy a double share of honor. You will possess a double portion of prosperity in your land, and everlasting joy will be yours*" (NLT).

5. Let's personalize this one too. Place your name in the blanks.

Instead of shame and dishonor, _____ will enjoy a double share of honor. _____ will possess a double portion of prosperity in [her] land, and everlasting joy will be _____ 's.

Do you believe this to be true for you? Can you grasp hold of the fact that Jesus has promised you a double portion of honor?

6. Write down a few things that you still feel are lacking honor in your marriage or personal life.

_____

_____

_____

_____

7. What are some things that you have not forgiven yourself for regarding to your marriage?

_____

_____

_____

_____

8. What are some fears or failures that continue to haunt you?

_____

_____

_____

_____

9. Read Acts 3:19 and write down the things that you must do so that the Lord can refresh your weary heart.

_____

_____

_____

_____

Take a few moments to pray with me and ask the Holy Spirit to help us receive forgiveness from our Redeemer and appropriate His honor into our lives.

> *Father,*
>
> *Thank You that You sent Your Son to die for us, taking our shame upon Himself and bearing in His bosom the reproach of many, as Psalm 89:50 tells us. I thank You because You have promised that if we follow You, trusting You fully and seeking Your kingdom above all else, You will restore a double portion of honor and prosperity to us, our husbands, and our marriages. Praise You, mighty King Jesus, that You have also promised to grant us everlasting joy here on earth and in heaven with You. Please teach us to grasp hold of these promises, believe You for them, and walk in the light of their glory, rather than in the darkness of shame and guilt. We ask these things in the name of Jesus. Amen.*

I pray that these truths will implant themselves deep in our hearts and that we may allow them to grow richly there, producing the fruit of joy and peace.

Let us now move to the forgiveness of our husbands. For some of us, this is an easier topic. For others, it is much more difficult. Please know that it is not easy for me either.

I fear that sometimes people look at my life and circumstances, hear my words (or in this case, read them), and feel that I am some kind of hero or super figure of a wife. Let me tell you right now, I am *not*. I am no hero, super wife, or stoic woman with the strength of steel. I have cried, screamed, and used horrible language at my husband. I have pouted, pounded the walls, cried myself to sleep, and sobbed in the shower. I have suffered in the deep dark valleys where I desired death over my pain.

But I have come out alive and joyful *because of Jesus*. Let me say this yet *again*: There is *no* healing apart from Jesus. My dear friend, time does *not* heal all wounds. *Jesus* heals all wounds. Time only allows distance, which is good and necessary, but it cannot heal the dark hidden places of sorrow and rejection that you and I have suffered—places within our hearts that no one else has ever seen and that you and I may not even know exist.

Only Jesus gets the glory for the fact that I, a woman of grace and forgiveness, sit here today. This is also true of you. You must find peace and wholeness in the arms of your Savior in order to fully forgive your husband.

I have had to broach this topic yet again in my own marriage this very week. After more than six years since the affair, things that burn my heart and sting my eyes still arise. This time for the sake of you and my husband and most importantly, for the cause of Christ, the Lord asked me to forgive this particular offense without approaching my husband regarding the pain that he had caused. I had to wrestle with the Lord on this one. I had to take it to Him, yell, scream, and ask, *Why? It's so unfair.*

Eventually, He brought me to the place where I had to simply lay it at the feet of Jesus and say, *Okay, if you won't let me confront him with this and express how painful it was, I need you to rebuke him for it. I need you to deal with his insufficiency and inconsistency.* The Holy Spirit then reminded me, "I desire mercy and not sacrifice" (Hosea 6:6 NKLV). Mercy displayed in quiet absolution is of greater value to my King than any gift I could think to give Him.

Let's search out what the Lord means by mercy and expects from us with regard to forgiveness, while keeping in mind the things that we have learned about the conscious choice to forgive.

10. Read the passages and write down what you learn.

Matthew 9:10–13

_____

_____

_____

_____

Daniel 9:8–9

_____

_____

_____

Matthew 6:14–15

_____

_____

_____

Matthew 18:21–35

_____

_____

_____

11. Which of these verses was most impactful to you? Why?

_____

_____

_____

_____

12. What choices or changes do you need to make in pursuit of forgiveness?

_____

_____

_____

_____

I want to take the last few minutes of our time today to do a little exercise. Use the next couple of pages to write down all the things you still struggle to forgive your husband for. Then cut out each one on the dotted line so that you have several smaller pages.

Next, burn each of them, one at a time (please use caution and be careful to do this in a safe place). As you burn them, pray that the Lord would help you forgive that particular offense and not bring it up in anger or resentment ever again—even if it's only in the secret places of your mind and heart. Then make the conscious choice to forgive that sin whether you feel like it or not. Choose to not allow that thing to continue to plague your marriage. If the thing does show up in your mind again, recall the moment you burned it and made the decision to release your husband from that offense.

At the beginning of the week, we discussed the holy standard that has been set before us to fear the Lord so that the life of Jesus may flow through us. In order to express our fear of Him in a practical way, we are commanded to remove deceit and evil speech from our lips and pursue peace. This includes the willful dismissal of anger and resentment that we still carry toward all those who have wounded us. We must choose forgiveness constantly and purposefully.

I really hope that you were able to write out the things that you had been holding against your husband, cut them out, pray over them, repent of them, and *burn* them. I pray that it was a blessing to both you and your husband (although he may never know how many cards you filled out) and that you were able to release him of all those wrongs.

Lastly, let us be ever purposeful in replacing evil thoughts and hurtful speech with glory and praise to our King. I pray that our hearts will be filled with gratitude and courage as we seek to make our homes a sanctuary of worship and joy.

Come, you children, listen to me;

I will teach you the fear of the Lord.

Who is the man who desires life

And loves length of days that he may see good?

Keep your tongue from evil

And your lips from speaking deceit.

Depart from evil and do good;

Seek peace and pursue it.

(Psalm 34:11–14)

Week 5

REDEMPTION
PSALM 34:15–22

In 2 Corinthians 11:2, Paul said that he was jealous for the people of Corinth because he was afraid that they would be deceived by the devil and stray away from their simple and pure devotion to Jesus. That is my concern for you also. After all the difficulty, trials, heartaches, and dirty feet, we have accomplished so much. My fear is that you will get tired because the journey is long, allow the enemy to woo you to sleep, or worse, turn aside from the path of healing.

I pray that you will continue forward, endure the rugged terrain and marshy valleys, and keep your eyes fixed on Jesus. We have not arrived at our destination as long as we breathe the air of this earth, but we are ever moving forward. This week as we focus on the truths of God, I pray that you will be ever mindful of the coming journey: the one that you will be making on your own without me. I pray that you will look for truths to keep hidden within your heart, which will enable you to dispel the deceptions of the enemy.

It is much harder to journey alone than with a friend. The enemy knows this. He will attempt to cause you to stumble. He will try to get you to turn back or to the side, but remember, dear one, you are never alone. Jesus, your Redeemer, is right beside you, holding your hand, and whispering to you. Open your ears to Him this week and let His words penetrate your heart, such that they may remain there when the road gets lonely.

DAY 1: CHOSEN, CALLED, AND BLESSED

Blessed be the God and Father of our Lord Jesus Christ, who has blessed us with every spiritual blessing in the heavenly places in Christ, just as He chose us in Him before the foundation of the world. (Ephesians 1:3)

As I've prepared to write this week's lesson, I've come under some heavy attacks from the enemy. He doesn't want me to write this, and he certainly doesn't want you to study it. He knows the climax for all that we have done together lies here as we approach our hearts' redemption.

In an effort to keep my hand from this keyboard, he has fed me all kinds of lies. The biggest and sadly the most effective lie has been that I am not worthy to be the one chosen to write this study. How could I be? I'm just a regular person, a mom, and a wife, who sometimes gets it right but most often, gets it all wrong. I'm grumpy, stubborn, lazy, and resentful. I tell myself that my marriage is healed and resurrected, but then there are days when I look at my heart and think, *Am I just fooling myself?*

Yet I have been reminded *again* by the precious whispers of the Holy Spirit through His word that I am "a chosen race, a royal priesthood, a holy nation, a people for God's own possession, so that [I] may proclaim the excellencies of Him who has called [me] out of darkness into His marvelous light" (1 Peter 2:9). I have been chosen to proclaim the excellence of God's faithfulness and His purpose for glory in your life and mine. I must replace the lies with these truths.

Perhaps you too have been wrestling with some of the enemy's lies about yourself and your marriage. Let's begin our lesson today with some quiet moments in prayer. Take a couple minutes to praise the Lord for His goodness and faithfulness. Then ask Him to reveal the lies that the enemy has been whispering into your mind. Just sit with your heart and mind being still before the Lord for a few moments and let Him speak. Be ever so careful to listen to all that He says. Sometimes there are deeply rooted lies hidden in the dark spider-webbed corners of our hearts, which only His Spirit can see.

1. Write down the lies that you are still believing, as the Holy Spirit reveals them to you.

_____

_____

_____

_____

Now let's take hold of God's truths and use them to dispel the enemy's lies. Open your Bible—the paper one that you can smell, touch, and hear as the pages turn. Read 1 Peter 2:4–10 and highlight or underline all the things that speak of who you are in Christ. Linger there awhile and mediate on those things.

Did you see all of them? Did you catch the one that talks about us being living stones built up into a spiritual house? Did you find the one that says you are a royal priest and a minister of the Lord Almighty? We have already discussed our position as the temple of the Holy Spirit and studied the truth of the King's very indwelling presence in our hearts, so let's take a few minutes to meditate on what it means to be a royal priesthood.

2. In Exodus 19:5–6, *Yahweh God calls the people who obey His voice and follow His call "a kingdom of* _____ *and a* _____ *nation."*

3. According to Exodus 28:1–4, to whom does a priest minister?

_____

_____

_____

_____

4. What does Leviticus 2:8–9 say are to be done with the sacrifices that are presented to the priest?

_____

_____

_____

_____

5. Leviticus 5:10, 16 states that the priest does what for the sins of others?

_____

_____

_____

_____

The priests of God prayed for the people and offered sacrifices on their behalves in order to atone for their sins. According to *Strong's Concordance*, atonement means, "To cover, purge, make reconciliation," for wrongs done against God.[39]

We know that according to Hebrews 2:17 and 5:10 that Jesus is the High Priest who makes atonement for the sins of all people. Hebrews 7:25 states that He makes intercession for all the saints. We have also learned that we are no longer to sacrifice animals, but our fully surrendered lives and our praises are the sacrifices God desires. We have Jesus, the ultimate priest, so none other is needed, and there is no need for more sacrifices to be made on our behalves.

So what does Peter mean when he calls us priests? We are anointed, chosen people of God. Although we cannot pay for the sins of others, we are still expected to act as priests interceding and atoning for them by our prayers. We are to make sacrifices of praise and petition before the Lord on their behalves. We implore our King to grant them mercy and repentance and for their ears to be attentive to His voice. In so doing, we are opening heaven to them in the spiritual realm.

6. Write what Paul says of his (and our) priestly responsibilities in Romans 15:16.

_____

_____

_____

_____

Paul considers the people themselves to be his sacrifice to the Lord. All his labors, prayers, sleepless nights, and turmoil are for the sake of presenting them to God as an offering (see 2 Corinthians 11:2). Remember that the animal had to be sacrificed on the altar and burned. If those whom we pray for are to be offered by us as sacrifices, they too must die. We are responsible for praying that they would be willing to do so. They will have to die to themselves and their own desires just as you and I have been learning to do. As is the case with the death and burning of a sacrifice, this might be quite painful for that person and possibly for us.

Oswald Chambers explains the priestly ministry of prayer in this way.

> True intercession involves bringing the person, or the circumstance that seems to be crashing in on you, before God, until you are changed by His attitude toward that person or circumstance. Intercession means to "fill up … [with] what is lacking in the afflictions of Christ" (Colossians 1:24), and this is precisely why there are so few intercessors.[40]

In order for our marriages to be healed, dear one, we must be willing to roll up our sleeves or jeans, as it were, get down on our knees, and pray. We must pray for the will of the Father in every circumstance of our lives and the lives of our husbands—no matter what the cost. Just as the people of Israel confessed their sins to the priests who prayed for them, we too must confess our sins to those believers whom we can be confident will pray God's mercy over us.

7. Once more, look at James 5:16. What are we to do to be healed?

_____

_____

_____

_____

Our position as the priests of God is probably one of the first ways the enemy attempts to lie to us, get us off track, and make us feel defeated. He gets us thinking, *This will never really get better. My husband can't truly be repentant. He'll probably do it again, and we'll be right back here again. I can't pray for him. I'm too angry at him. What good will it do anyway?* Does any of that sound familiar? How about this one, *Is God even really listening? After all, He is the One who allowed all this in the first place. Why would He bother caring now?*

It is necessary that we cling to the truths in scripture. By these alone are we able to "resist the devil and he will flee" from us (James 4:7). So let's continue dissecting the identity that Peter reminded us is ours.

8. Read 1 Peter 2:9 again. Place your name on the first line, then enter on the next line all the things that Peter said Christ has made you.

_____ is _____.

_____ is _____.

_____ is _____.

_____ is _____.

_____ is _____.

9. Now read Ephesians 1:3–8 and do the same exercise.

_____ is _____.

_____ is _____.

_____ is _____.

_____ is _____.

_____'s King has freely bestowed grace upon her

_____ has _____ through the blood of Jesus

and _____ according to the grace,

which is lavished on _____.

Jesus has cleansed you, made you right before the Father, and given you His glory and His light. He has set you as a royal priest (to pray and intercede). Before the foundation of the world, He chose you to be the object of His lavish grace.

If all that weren't already enough (which it is), remember that He blessed us according to Ephesians 1:3, with every spiritual blessing in the heavenly places. That means the blessings of the Spirit of God are ours for the keeping. According to David Guzik, they are "far better than material blessings. These blessings are ours in the heavenly places in Christ, they are higher, better, and more secure than earthly blessings."[41] We don't attain them because we deserve them or have somehow worked to earn them. The blessings of our King are freely given to us so that we may be a blessing to others.

Charles Spurgeon reminds us that spiritual blessings come in the form of a new heart—one that is able to love others and not only itself. We obtain Jesus as our food and portion for all fulfillment, physically, emotionally, and spiritually.[42] We have been given the gifts of the Holy Spirit and freedom from the slavery of sin—the slavery that condemns us to constantly betray our true nature as God's image bearers.

Many of us are unaware that gifts of the Holy Spirit are present in our lives or we often neglect to ask our Father to enable us to properly employ them. Some of us have never asked. But Jesus said in Luke 11:13 … well, why don't you read it for yourself.

10. *"If you then, being _____, know how to give _____ gifts to your children, how much _____ will your heavenly Father give the _____ to those who ask Him?"*

Jesus said that all we have to do is ask, and the Holy Spirit will be given to us. Lest we forget or become somehow disillusioned with God, let us remind ourselves again that He is *good*. He is perfect and faithful in His goodness. No matter what the circumstance or how horrific or torturous it is, God, our Father and the Creator who formed and loves us, is *good*.

We are evil, yet we love and care for our children and do not withhold the necessities of life from them. How much more will our good God lavish His Spirit upon us if we ask? With the presence of His Spirit being there, won't He then add to us the fruit, or attributes as we might call them, of Himself to our lives? Let's take a minute to look at the gifts of the Spirit, which are available to us in Jesus.

11. Read Galatians 5:22–25 and list the character qualities that His Spirit will produce in us when we are seeking His presence in our lives.

1._____   2._____

3._____   4._____

5._____   6._____

7._____   8._____

9._____

Isn't it such a relief to know that we don't have to produce goodness or self-control within ourselves? Have you ever tried? I keep trying to get my five-year-old to practice self-control and feel like I'm hitting my head against a wall. One day last week, I realized that I was asking her to do the impossible. She couldn't manufacture self-control, especially when she wasn't seeing it displayed by others in the home (this is where I would insert the embarrassed emoji).

I began praying that the Lord would restore my own self-control so that I might be an example to her. Then I began praying *with* her that the Father would grant us both the self-control that He had promised. Life has been much more pleasant this week. God is truly good.

12. List some spiritual blessings that should ask the Father to impart to you as you continue to seek healing in your marriage.

_____

_____

_____

_____

13. *Write out* the truths that ministered to you the most today, on the next page. Then cut out that portion of the page and hang it in your kitchen or on your bathroom mirror to remind you to dwell upon those things throughout the rest of the week.

You will know the truth, and the truth will make you free. (John 8:32)

_____

_____

_____

_____

I pray that you will be emboldened and encouraged throughout this week to claim the truths of God and the promises that are yours in His Spirit. I pray that they will be continually implanted in your heart and mind and that their fruit will be evident in your life.

- -

DAY 2: THE KING JUDGES THE WICKED

Arise, O Lord! Save me, O my God! For you strike all my enemies
on the cheek; you break the teeth of the wicked. (Psalm 3:7)

I have moved this topic repeatedly. I tried to place it in one day's study or another and purposefully avoided it in others. Now it is time to address it. This is our final week. We can no longer hide from the reality of the other woman in our hearts and marriages.

I am keenly aware that you may have read that last sentence and have been tempted to skip today's lesson. I implore you, however, to come with me one last time into the dense fog of the low valley. We will tread lightly, being careful not to become stuck in the mud. Once more, we must compel our hearts to take courage as we duck under the branches of thick trees and journey on through the dark forest.

We know we are supposed to forgive our husbands. We have spent a great deal of time discussing our hearts toward them, but what about the women who they betrayed us with? What are we to do with them?

What is our Judge's heart regarding the women whom we consider our enemies? Could it be that He expects us to offer unsought (and frankly undeserved) forgiveness toward them as well? Let's jump into His Word with open hearts and willing minds. But before we do, why don't you pray with me.

Father,

You are so good. We know that You have been faithful and kind as we have journeyed along this winding, dusty, and sometimes excruciating path. Our hearts pale and shrink back as we look at the road that is still ahead of us. Yet again, please go before us and prepare a straight path. Give our hearts courage and peace. Please grant us mercy and forgiveness toward our enemies and if necessary, even repentance. Please enable us to hear from You by making our hearts ever attentive to Your Spirit today. In the name of Jesus, for Your glory we ask this.

Now let's look up and read Luke 12:41–48.

1. What does Peter ask Jesus? What is Jesus's response?

_____

_____

_____

_____

2. How do you think this passage applies to you and me (in a general sense)?

_____

_____

_____

_____

3. In what ways do you think it applies to our topic for today?

_____

_____

_____

_____

Peter asked Jesus if this parable was only for the disciples, the chosen few, or if it included those surrounding them.

In this scene, Jesus and His disciples were pressed in by a great crowd, but it appears when He first sat down to speak that it was directed only toward the twelve (see Luke 12:1). However at some point, Jesus began speaking to a larger circle.

We can't assume to know what Peter was thinking or feeling at this point, but surely, he must have been somewhat confused when Jesus said in verse 40, "The Son of Man is coming at an hour that you do not expect." He probably thought, *But you are already here, and we know it is you.*

However, Jesus spoke to Peter as gently and graciously as He does to you and me, asking, "Who is the faithful one who will do as I have asked?" (paraphrase mine, see Luke 12:42-44). In other words, He is giving Peter the opportunity to figure out for himself to whom the command is being spoken. He says what might sound to us like, "Peter, I am speaking to the person who will listen and obey." The choice belongs to the person who is listening. That person must decide whether the message was meant for him or her.

Jesus asks the same question of us, "Daughter, will you also be the one to whom I am speaking?" He prods, "Will you be the faithful steward, whom has been given much, and who is willing to bless rather than beat her fellow servants with anger and bitterness? Or will you become drunk on self-pity and resentment?"

Jesus said, "From everyone who has been given much, much will be required; and to whom they entrusted much, of him they will ask all the more" (Luke 12:48). My dear sister, haven't you and I been given *so* much? We have a Redeemer who loves us and sets us free. He descended from His throne to become a curse for us. He paid all our debts in full and remains in our hearts so that we may call upon Him at any moment and for any reason. Isn't that cause enough for us to fall on our faces and ask, *What do you desire of me? Whatever it is, I will do it.*

Yet there's more, isn't there? He gave us a marriage back from the dead and a husband who is repentant and desires to set things right. He has given us life and breath in our lungs. We have a purpose, a calling, a role to play in His story, and the hope of heaven for when this life is done. We can give the gift of forgiveness because we have been forgiven.

4. Write what Jesus says in Matthew 9:10–13 about God's desire for us.

But go and learn what this means: "I desire _____*, and not* _____*," for I did not come to call the righteous, but sinners.*

5. In our present culture, who are the sinners spoken of in verse 10?

_____

_____

_____

6. In Matthew 6:14–15, what does Jesus tell us will prevent us from being forgiven by the Father?

_____

_____

_____

7. Write James 2:10–14 in your own words.

_____

_____

_____

8. Explain what you think Proverbs 25:21–22 means for followers of Jesus.

_____

_____

_____

_____

9. Do the above passages offer *any* exclusions for our forgiveness? (Circle one)

Yes, one.

No, none.

I imagine that that one hurt quite a bit. It was painful for me as well. Tears well up in my eyes as I ponder my capacity (or incapacity) to truly be able to forgive her.

My husband walked into the room while I was writing that last section and asked about dinner. I was so grateful for the interruption. However, I'm not sure he was ready for the fallout that I unloaded, which had built up in my heart over the past two pages. Poor guy. But he took my tears and frustrated discourse like a champ.

No one but no one should be considered unworthy of our forgiveness. Just as Jesus condemned the evil servants for not being watchful of their master's coming, so He condemns our demands for our own rights. His heart is for our freedom, and He knows we cannot be free if we are clutching desperately to our own rights, vengeance, and vindication. He requires that we let go of these unhealthy attitudes and surrender to His authority, trusting that His purposes for us and for *her* are greater than our own. Look again at our theme verse for today and the passage it comes from (Psalm 3:1–8).

10. Write how David's feelings echo your own.

_____

_____

_____

_____

There's so much packed into this little psalm. We could talk about so much, but I would like to focus on just a couple of key things. First, did you see in the introduction that David wrote this when he was fleeing from his *son*? If you're not familiar with the story, you can look it up in 2 Samuel 15:1–37. David's own son had set his mind on overthrowing his father and taking over the kingdom. Absalom betrayed his father, "stole away" the hearts of the people, and planned to take David's crown by force. So David fled, and in the midst of this betrayal and the fear for his own life, David pens this song.

> *But You, O Lord, are a shield about me,*
> *My glory, and the One who lifts my head.*
> *I was crying to the Lord with my voice,*
> *And He answered me from His holy mountain. Selah.*
> *I lay down and slept;*
> *I awoke, for the Lord sustains me.*
> *I will not be afraid of ten thousands of people*
> *Who have set themselves against me round about.* (Psalm 3:3-6)

The king was in fear for his life, yet he was able to lie down, sleep, and awake again in peace because his hope and trust were in the Lord. Just as David found rest for his soul in the presence of *his* King, you and I can cry out to our Redeemer, and we are given solace and the peace that surpasses all understanding. Look carefully, though, at what David says next.

> *Arise, O Lord; Save me, O my God.*
> *For You have struck all my enemies on the cheekbone;*
> *You have broken the teeth of the ungodly.*
> *Salvation belongs to the Lord.*
> *Your blessing is upon Your people. Selah* (Psalm 3:7–8 NKJV).

The Lord has struck David's enemies on the cheekbone? That's right. God flat-out punched them in the face and broke their teeth. Wouldn't you like to walk up to the woman who taunted and tempted your husband to betray you and punch her in the face?

There certainly was a point in time when I wanted to that very thing. In fact, I nearly did one day. By the grace of God, I decided against it, but to my shame, I did choose to spew venomous, nasty words, which I regret to this day. My prayer is that you won't follow my example but that you will recognize the incredible power of your King to strike your enemy where He—the One who knows all things, even to the very depths of her heart—knows it will hurt the most. Rather than taking our own revenge or saying something to elicit an apology (albeit a fake one) or gain some sort of victory in our own minds, you and I are better off trusting the true Judge of all the earth to be the one who strikes our enemies in the face.

In Deuteronomy 32, the Lord reminds us,

"Is it not laid up in store with Me,
Sealed up in My treasuries?
"Vengeance is Mine, and retribution,
In due time their foot will slip;
For the day of their calamity is near,
And the impending things are hastening upon them …
See now that I, I am He,
And there is no god besides Me;
It is I who put to death and give life.
I have wounded and it is I who heal,
And there is no one who can deliver from My hand.
'Indeed, I lift up My hand to heaven,
And say, as I live forever,
If I sharpen My flashing sword,
And My hand takes hold on justice,
I will render vengeance on My adversaries,
And I will repay those who hate Me.
"I will make My arrows drunk with blood,
And My sword will devour flesh,
With the blood of the slain and the captives,
From the long-haired leaders of the enemy." (Deuteronomy 32:34–35 and
39–42)

Our King is not lax or forgetful. He will collect on what is due Him, and He will make those who have harmed us pay. It's perfectly natural to want revenge and retribution, but Jesus has much greater in mind than you and I could fathom for repayment of the wrongs that have been done to us. I do not believe that it's wrong for us to pray for the retribution of our wounds.

King David also prayed for God to judge his enemies, but let's be careful to follow his example entirely.

11. Read Psalm 55:12–23 and note all that David says about those who have betrayed him.

_____

_____

_____

_____

12. Reread verses 22–23 and fill in the blanks.

"Cast your _____ *upon the Lord and He will* _____ *you; He will* _____ *allow the righteous to be shaken. But You, O God, will bring* _____
                                                                            (her name)

*down to the pit of destruction; [Women] of bloodshed and deceit will not live out half their days. But*_____ *will* _____*in [Jesus]."*

13. Look again at Psalm 34:16–21 and express God's plans for the evil doers.

_____

_____

_____

_____

You and I are free to forgive because we can trust that greater judgment lies with our Holy God, "who is able to destroy both soul and body in hell" (Matthew 10:28). In fact, we ought to tremble on behalf of all those whom the Judge will not be merciful toward. As Jesus tells us in Matthew 10:28, we should fear *Him* more than anyone on earth. We should pray for those who must face His wrath. The writer of Hebrews reminds us, "It is a terrifying thing to fall into the hands of the living God" (Hebrews 10:31).

I pray that we may be able to forgive these women who have wounded us and pray for God's mercy to fall on them so that they will be granted repentance before Him. Truly, isn't that the ultimate revenge? It is for a broken, ashamed, and repentant woman to fall on her face before a Holy God and cry out for mercy. That is what I long to see for all my enemies: true repentance, sorrow, and the glory of my King wrapped around them in royal white robes, just as He has wrapped me in the corner of His garment. Remember that we don't deserve it any more than they do.

Before we end for the day, let's take a moment to pray for our own hearts. Let's pray that they would soften toward the Lord's commands and pray for repentance of unforgiveness. Let's also pray for the hearts of those who have betrayed us. Write your prayer in the margin if you wish.

If you're still struggling with or unsettled about this topic, I highly recommend that you pour over Psalms. There are many places where David cries out against his enemies. Find peace beyond understanding there in the Word of God. You might also pick up a copy of Erwin Lutzer's book *When You've been Wronged*. He unwraps the difficult feelings and hard-to-pinpoint causes of our struggles while giving down-to-earth guidance for navigating the process of forgiveness.

DAY 3: WHAT IS REDEMPTION?

The Lord Jesus Christ, who gave Himself for our sins so that He might rescue us from this present evil age, according to the will of our God and Father. (Galatians 1:3–4)

As we round the corner of our last week together, we look into the future and wonder what will come of all that is behind us. We look expectantly at what lies ahead, yet we wonder, *Will it ever really be set right?*

Our Redeemer wants us to know with confidence that He walks before us, beside us, behind us. "You have enclosed me behind and before, And [You have] placed Your hand upon me" (Psalm 139:5 AMP). He has ordained all that we have experienced so that we might be taught to know Him. He fully intends to make it *all* right again. For some of us, that may not come until we reach His arms in heaven, but we'll talk about that tomorrow.

Do It Again[43]

Walking around these walls
I thought by now they'd fall
But You have never failed me yet
Waiting for change to come
Knowing the battle's won
For You have never failed me yet
...

I know the night won't last
Your Word will come to pass
My heart will sing Your praise
again

Whether we experience complete restoration in our marriages and the wholeness of our lives here on earth or the King has greater plans of a higher glory not realized until we arrive in His house, we all have the opportunity to experience the glory of having our hearts healed in the here and now. His purpose for you and me, dear friend, is that we know the joy and beauty of His redemption.

1. Read Colossians 2:13–14 and note what Jesus has done for you.

_____

_____

_____

_____

Our Redeemer was nailed to the cross, and the "certificate of debt consisting of legal demands [which were in force] against us and which were hostile to us" so that we might be free (Colossians 2:14 AMP). Think of it. It's as if every sin—from the little white lie you told your parents as a young kid to the most hideous form of idolatry—was written on a promissory note that had to be paid. It bore your signature and acknowledged your debt. It was simply nailed to the cross. Jesus hung it there and just walked away, leaving the note behind. He would never come asking for repayment or bring it to your attention again. He paid it himself.

It would be as if the president of Chase Bank took your $100 trillion loan and said, "I got this one. Your account is closed."

However, we know it wasn't that easy. Jesus didn't just show up with the hammer, nail the thing up there, and walk away. He wasn't the one holding the hammer at all, and He didn't walk away. He was carried—beaten, bloody, and lifeless—to a tomb. The payment was unspeakable. Yet His Father decided that you are worth it. Together, they willingly paid such an outrageous ransom for you and me so that we may live in communion with them.

So too, they desire our marriages to experience the same communion. Our Redeemer paid our debts and those of our husbands in order to make a path from anger and bitterness to joy and enraptured love.

2. Look up the word _communion_ in the dictionary. What does it say?

_____

_____

_____

_____

The *Oxford Dictionary* defines communion this way: "The sharing or exchanging of intimate thoughts and feelings, especially when the exchange is on a mental or spiritual level."[44] And our hearts leap as we say, "Yes!" Isn't that what we so intensely long for in our lives and marriages?

3. In what ways is your marriage in need of deeper communion?

_____

_____

_____

_____

Jesus's desire for our marriages is that we experience this deep kind of fellowship with our husbands. Redemption means that the King came down, paid our debts, and restored us, not only to where we were before but also to something greater. He gave us a higher form of intimacy with God, a deeper commitment, and enjoyment of our spouses—a greater glory than we could have imagined.

In Leviticus 27:11–27, the Lord was giving directions to help the Hebrews understand redemption. They had to set apart a certain amount of land and animals to God as they honored their duty to Him. However, they could redeem or buy them back under strict parameters.

4. Read Leviticus 27:15, 19 and note the cost of redemption.

> To redeem his house a man must add _____ percent to its value.
>
> To redeem his field, he must add _____ percent to its value.

The cost of redeeming the land or the house required a person to add value to the property. Remember with me that all of God's laws serve a greater purpose than trying to control the behavior of His people. They are designed to point us to His greater mission and the greater glory: the redemption of humanity. If property must increase in value when it is redeemed, how much more will our lives, souls, marriages, and families increase in value when they are redeemed?

Our King has called us to mercy, forgiveness, sexual pleasure, and deeper intimacy for one purpose only: to display His plan of redemption (greater glory) to the world. We have the privilege of being made an example of His value and glory, which He has stamped on our lives. He desires to take the marriage we had before and restore it to more than what it was. Then He adds the power of our new testimony to it, making it more beautiful, alluring, and enduring than ever. The beautiful thing about redemption is that it takes something ugly, filthy, wretched, and broken and makes it lovely, whole, and glorious (shining with the holiness of Jesus).

5. Read the passages in Isaiah and add your name to all the blanks.

I have wiped out _____'s transgressions like a thick cloud
And your sins like a heavy mist.
Return to Me, for I have redeemed _____.
Shout for joy, O heavens, for the Lord has done it!
Shout joyfully, you lower parts of the earth;
Break forth into a shout of joy, you mountains,
O forest, and every tree in it;
For the Lord has redeemed _____
And in _____ He shows forth His glory. (Isaiah 44:22–23)
Listen! Your watchmen lift up their voices,
Together they shout for joy;
For they will see face to face
The return of the Lord to _____.
Break forth, shout joyfully together,
You ruins of _____;
For the Lord has comforted His people,
He has redeemed _____.
The Lord has bared His holy arm (His infinite power)
Before the eyes of all the nations [revealing Himself as the One by Whom _____ is redeemed from captivity],
That all the ends of the earth may see
The salvation of our God. (Isaiah 52:8–10 AMP)

6. What themes do you see running through both of these passages?

_____

_____

_____

_____

7. How do these passages speak life into your marriage?

_____

_____

_____

_____

"That all the ends of the earth may see the salvation [the greatness of our King's graciousness toward us] of our God" (Isaiah 52:10). His desire is to see us shout for joy and worship His goodness and faithfulness. Whether we are led to share our stories with others or not, we are given redemption in order to bring honor and praise to the name of Jesus.

Psalm 107:2 says, "Let the redeemed of the Lord say so, Whom He has redeemed from the hand of the adversary." The Bible says we are to proclaim all that has been done for us— the recovery of our ability to maintain a gentle-hearted conversation with our husbands, the forgiveness of the other woman, and complete restoration of our hearts to wholeness. We are to sing for the things that He will *continue* to do as we praise, worship, and pray in faith.

8. Look at Galatians 4:5–7 and highlight what Jesus has made you.

> *So that He might redeem those who were under the Law, that we might receive the adoption as [daughters]. Because you are [daughters], God has sent forth the Spirit of His Son into our hearts, crying, "Abba! Father!" Therefore you are no longer a slave, but a [daughter]; and if a [daughter], then an heir through God.*

Instead of slavery, we have been given daughterhood and the joy of an inheritance from the King (His Kingdom and glory). But even better than that, we get to experience it here on earth. The joy, peace, and grace of heaven dwell within our hearts and homes by the power of the Holy Spirit. We *shine* with His beauty as we live out this legacy of grace.

9. Spend some time reflecting on the areas of your marriage or your own heart that have already experienced greater glory. Share your thoughts.

_____

_____

_____

_____

It is imperative that we understand that our marriages will never be perfect this side of heaven. We will still have trials, arguments, anger, and miscommunication. There are plenty of opportunities for two broken, sinful people to hurt each other, and none of them will have anything to do with our wounds. Hear me.

Your husband will hurt you, possibly often, but not because of his betrayal. Rather, it's simply because he is a sinner and a man. He is only a man. Remember that he can't possibly understand the complexity and vulnerability that it is to be you—a woman. It's essential to identify his failings (and your own) as everyday insufficiencies, without associating them with his betrayal.

Sometimes we think that once we've been healed of this wound, we will magically have perfect marriages. This is simply impossible.

10. List some unrealistic expectations that you have about what life and marriage will be like after you have healed. Then pray to cast them out of your mind.

_____

_____

_____

_____

I want to spend the last few minutes of our time together discussing what our Redeemer has said about the husband who hasn't yet experienced His grace. Some of us have had the difficulty of husbands who have been repentant toward us but not toward the Lord. It can be terribly frightening to think that they might betray us again, particularly when they have not surrendered their lives to Jesus. Even for those of us who have husbands who do love Jesus, there is still a great deal of turmoil in our hearts over whether or not they have fully submitted their addictions, lust, or selfishness to God's authority.

11. Carefully read Acts 2:38–39 and note who will receive forgiveness and the gift of the Holy Spirit. Circle your answer.

> Myself
>
> My children
>
> All of my household including those who are far off

Peter said that none is too far off to receive the forgiveness of sins. The first several times that I read this, my thought was that he was talking about those who lived far away. But I don't believe that's entirely the meaning of Peter's statement. What happens to those husbands who are far away spiritually, emotionally, or mentally from seeking the mercy offered to them? Are they excluded from God's invitation? No. Jesus has made Himself and His Holy Spirit available to "all who are far off" (Acts 2:39).

When we pray for our husbands and their struggles, whether they are addictions or hatred of God Himself, we must pray with absolute confidence that Jesus will save them. He said that they are *not* too far away. *No one* is too far from His reach.

We need to pray with this verse in mind, recite it back to the Father, and remind Him that He has said that this "promise is for [us] and [our] children and for all who are far off, as many as the Lord our God will call to Himself" (Acts 2:39). I must confess that when I read that last phrase, I wondered, *But who will He call to Himself?* Do you find yourself wondering the same thing? It's okay to ask Jesus the big questions, remember? He can handle it. Let's ask Him and see what His Word says in response.

12. Read and underline what is said about God's heart toward those who are far off.

Romans 11:31–32

So these also now have been disobedient, that because of the mercy shown to you they also may now be shown mercy. For God has shut up all in disobedience so that He may show mercy to all.

1 Timothy 2:4

This is good and acceptable in the sight of God our Savior, who desires all men to be saved and to come to the knowledge of the truth. For there is one God, and one mediator also between God and men, the man Christ Jesus.

Amos 9:11–12

"In that day I will restore the fallen house of David. I will repair its damaged walls. From the ruins I will rebuild it and restore its former glory. And Israel will possess what is left of Edom and all the nations I have called to be mine." The Lord has spoken, and he will do these things.
(**NLT**)

I love the passage in Amos because it so beautifully fits our study for today and not just this final topic. Read it one more time, replacing the words *David* and *Israel* with your own name.

It's also worth noting what the New Living Translation says the Greek version reads, "And restore its former glory, / so that the rest of humanity, including the Gentiles— / all those I have called to be mine—might seek me" (Amos 9:11–12). It says the "rest of humanity." This is all people whom the King has called to be His. None is forgotten, lost, or neglected. The Father is in absolute control.

He knows the heart of your husband, and He has promised to restore your fallen house and repair your walls. The new walls and the glory being restored will look different for each of us, but we are given a great deal of comfort in these passages. The desire of our King is to have all men come to the knowledge of the truth. So pray, dear one, and don't give up. No husband is too far off.

DAY 4: LIGHT IN THE DARKNESS

While we look not at the things which are seen, but at the things which are not seen; for the things which are seen are temporal, but the things which are not seen are eternal. (2 Corinthians 4:18)

At the risk of seeming contradictory, I feel compelled to address the extremely challenging topic of divorce. My prayer is that today's journey is a valley of struggle for me but a hilltop of peace for you.

Unfortunately, no matter how much we fast, pray, seek the Lord's wisdom and strength, or pour ourselves out for His purpose, some of our marriages will not survive the fall. It grieves me to no end that I must trek this terrain, but for the sake of those to whom it applies, please hear my heart and the heart of our King. God is sovereign over *all* these struggles. His purposes are still *good* and we *can* trust all that He is doing.

Father,

Please arrest our hearts with Your compassion for us and fill our minds with the truth of Your Word. Please make Your purposes for us as clear as they can be on this side of eternity so that we would know without a doubt that You are good and worthy of our trust. In Jesus's name, we humbly ask, amen.

We have discussed the sovereignty of the King, learned of His incredible power to save, and sought out His heart toward those who are far off, but one question remains: What happens to the ones who continue to persist in sin and rebellion? Does the despair of our marriages in the darkest places mean that the Redeemer is not present or that He has lost sight of our circumstances? Does it indicate that we are left alone to fend for ourselves? Or worse, does it mean that the Father has deemed us unworthy to receive His glory?

Let me tell you right now, lovely daughter, the resounding answer to all of these is, "No!" Our King has not forgotten us. His power is not diminished by our husbands' rebellion, and He has not decided that we (or our husbands) are too far-gone. Jesus is *still* King. He is *still* on the throne. His purposes for your life, the lives of your children, and the life of your husband are far greater than you and I can comprehend.

1. Read 1 Corinthians. 2:9–10 and write what it means for you and your marriage.

_____

_____

_____

_____

Regardless of the outcome, the God of heaven has plans for us that are greater than you or I could ever fathom. He has promised that He will reveal them to us by the power of the Holy Spirit (see 1 Corinthians. 2:10).

We already know the story of Job. We've discussed it before. We know how the Lord allowed Satan to kill all of Job's animals, his children, and all but four of his servants. Take a moment to imagine it with me. In a matter of minutes, your entire world crashes in. Well, you don't have to imagine it. I know you have already been there. But ponder how it must have felt to experience all that Job lost.

All your wealth is burnt in a house fire or lost in the stock market, your children are killed by a tornado, and your most precious friends are slain in a car accident. Even your dog is dead. I cannot fathom the agony of losing even one of my children, let alone all of them. That amount of shock and grief would be absolutely consuming. I can imagine Job not being able to get up off the ground for days, unable to eat, or to sleep, being tormented by the question, *Why?* Yet look at how he responded to it all.

> *Then Job arose and tore his robe and shaved his head, and he fell to the*
> *ground and worshiped. He said,*
> *"Naked I came from my mother's womb,*
> *And naked I shall return there.*
> *The Lord gave and the Lord has taken away.*
> *Blessed be the name of the Lord."*
> *Through all this Job did not sin nor did he blame God. (Job 1:20–22)*

Job did not blame God. Wow! I know I've had my fair share of blaming God. Haven't you? Yet in the midst of the immeasurable loss, which was by the hand of God when He gave all that Job had into Satan's power (see Job 1:12), not only did Job not blame God, but he also worshiped God. Job acknowledged the sovereign power of the King to give *and* to take away as He freely chose to.

That's pretty hard to swallow, isn't it? Imagine you and me responding to our King in that same manner, acknowledging God's absolute control, and trusting His intentions. I'm willing to bet that our lives would be *so* much richer.

As if it weren't enough for poor Job to have lost everything, God again prompts Satan, saying, "Have you considered My servant Job? For there is no one like him on the earth, a blameless and upright man ... he still holds fast his integrity, although you incited Me against him to ruin him without cause" (Job 2:3).

Before we discuss Job's response, there's something here I don't want you to miss. Did you see what God said? He stated that He Himself ruined Job "without a cause." He admits responsibility for Job's turmoil. He even acknowledges that there was no cause for it. Can you even comprehend that?

As the creator and sovereign supervisor of all the earth, the King of the universe asserts His power to stop Satan at any given moment. He had every right and capability to tell Satan, "No, you cannot attack my servant. He is righteous and has done no wrong." However, God does not do that, but He actually entreats Satan, saying, "Have you considered my servant Job?" When Satan accuses God of protecting Job too much, the Sovereign responds, "You think I'm playing favorites? Okay, go ahead. Give it your best shot. Let him prove for himself that his heart is wholly mine." I wonder whether God said the same of you and me prior to Satan ransacking our marriages.

Although we can't begin to understand the reason why, the *good* King releases all Job has yet again, into Satan's hand, including his own body. Again, Job does not get angry with God. Rather, he tells his wife, "Shall we indeed accept good from God and not accept adversity?" (Job 2:10). Again, Job recognizes the right of the Creator to rule the universe in any way that He chooses and with no input from those whom He has created. Job essentially says, "You and I are but dust, and God is absolutely sovereign." This means that He owns the rights to all His creation to do whatever He pleases with it. We, being dust, have no right to tell Him how to rule.

2. What has your honest response to God been in the midst of your trial?

_____

_____

_____

3. What still keeps you from saying, "Bless the name of the Lord"?

_____

_____

_____

4. What can you do to begin expressing your trust in God's goodness and sovereignty in spite of the circumstances?

_____

_____

_____

Let's look at another person who lost someone very dear to him. King David was told by the prophet Nathan that because of David's own sin, his new baby son was going to die. Can you imagine knowing that you had caused the death of your child?

Not only that, but the death should have been David's own death, according to the Law of Moses. Exodus 21:12 says, "He who strikes a man so that he dies shall surely be put to death." David, who studied God's law, knew as soon as Nathan had revealed his sin that the penalty was death. Yet Nathan said, "The Lord has forgiven you, and you won't die for this sin." For a brief moment, there must have been relief in David's heart.

The statement that came in the second breath must have made David wish that God had simply slain him: "Nevertheless … your child will die" (2 Samuel 12:13). What deep guilt and shame must have come from the knowledge that he had purposefully chosen evil, he had tried to cover it up, and his son would die as the punishment for David's own wickedness. Read the rest of the story in 2 Samuel 12:15–23.

5. What was David's response to God's proclamation against his son?

_____

_____

_____

_____

6. What did David do when God did not answer his prayer by healing the child?

_____

_____

_____

_____

David's first response was prayer. He poured himself out before the Lord in prayer and fasting, lying on the cold hard ground for what appears to be days. He "begged God to spare the child," while knowing what had already been declared. It seems obvious that David believed God could change His mind.

However, this is a concept that often eludes us. At least, it eludes me. We read scriptures that say, "God is not a man that He should lie, or a son of man that He should change His mind" (Numbers 23:19 ESV) and "He also is wise and will bring disaster, And does not retract His words, But will arise against the house of evildoers" (Isaiah 31:2), and we think, *How could a God like that be expected to go back on what He has declared?*

Yet, David seemed very confident that it was not out of God's character to relent from the calamity that He had proclaimed. It seems that David was familiar with the passages or at least the concepts of God, which state, "So the Lord changed His mind about the harm which He said He would do to His people" (Exodus 32:14), and, "I knew that You are a gracious and compassionate God, slow to anger and abundant in lovingkindness, and one who relents concerning calamity" (Jonah 4:2). He must have believed God's power to heal and His willingness to withdraw judgment.

Clearly, David also believed in miracles. He was a man of deep faith who loved His King. Surely, He believed strongly enough to prompt God to do the impossible. Yet the child still died.

It is common in some Christian circles for people to make statements rebuking God's servants for their lack of faith. They claim that had a person possessed a greater abundance of faith, the circumstances would not have ended poorly. Obviously, it was not a lack of faith on David's part that resulted in the loss of his son.

Rather than getting angry, blaming God, crying out against himself, or lamenting his own lack of faith when the child died, David got up, went to church, and worshiped his Creator. He praised His God.

This is such an extremely difficult thing for us to do. I wrestle so much with the knowledge that my King is worthy of worship, even when things turn out terribly (or at least what seems terribly to me). I must admit, my faith waivers and I struggle to believe that anything good can come of the trials that are before me or those whom I care about.

One such trial was that of a very dear friend who loved Jesus more than anyone I had ever met. Her husband appeared to love Jesus. They served together in the worship band for several years, helped start a new church, and counseled others in God's Word.

Needless to say, many who knew them were devastated when her husband up and left one day. He left her and their children for another woman and a lifestyle of drugs, alcohol, and womanizing, which he'd been battling and attempting to hide for many years. The grief was so deep that she didn't eat or sleep for months. She prayed and prayed. We prayed and prayed with her. Nothing changed. She felt the Lord release her of the bonds of this marriage, and she filed for divorce. We all grieved with her.

Over time, the Lord brought her a new husband. She is now happily married to a man who cherishes and adores her. They are extremely blessed in so many areas of life, just as Job was more blessed in his latter life. Oh, but I'm getting ahead of myself.

Open your Bible back up to Job and read Job 42:10–17. Note what our Redeemer did in Job's latter years.

7. Job had _____ more sons, _____ more daughters, he had more money, more livestock and was _____ blessed in his latter years than the _____.

Let's also return to David and see what God's purposes were for him in the midst of his great sorrow.

8. Read 2 Samuel 12:24–25 and 1 Chronicles 28:3–7 and note the outcome of David's story.

_____

_____

_____

_____

9. What do you believe was the reason for both Job's calamity and David's unanswered prayers?

_____

_____

_____

_____

I hope you answered, "For a greater glory, yet unseen." As we have been discovering, our King never has just one purpose in mind. His workings always result in our good, His own glory, and a greater glory for ourselves and those around us.

God took David's son, but He gave him Solomon in return. Solomon, the one who was "Beloved of the Lord" and became the richest, most famous, and wisest man to ever walk the earth (see 2 Samuel 12:25 and 2 Chronicles 1:12). What David received as an inheritance and a legacy in Solomon was far greater than what the son of David's sin could have ever been. Solomon was also the king through whom our own King would be born. Jesus is a descendant of Solomon.

Notice that Solomon was also a son of Bathsheba, the forbidden, adulterous woman and the wife of David's sin. Now she was a queen and the mother of the future king. What an incredible story of redemption for her. Because of her sin, Bathsheba's son died, and she should have been stoned to death. She certainly had no place in the kingdom of God's righteous people, yet she became the woman through whom the Savior was born. The sin and sorrowful consequences are replaced with a greater glory for both David and his wife. Isn't our Redeemer relentless?

I don't tell you this so that you'll be encouraged that another better life is out there than the one you're currently living or to excuse a self-centered mindset leaning toward divorce. I express all this so that you may know that if you have done all you can do, prayed all you can pray, and sought the Lord with all that is in you and nothing has changed in your husband, Jesus, your Redeemer, is still in control. His plans for you are *still good*.

My dear friend held onto her husband and her marriage and continued to pray right up until the divorce was filed. She believed God for a miracle and trusted that He would show her one. She did not give up, but she waited for her King to answer her pleas. He eventually did, but it was not in the way that she had originally hoped for. It was better.

When we pray, we need to pray as David did: believing that God will hear us and restore that which is broken. With all faith, all hope, and all joy, we accept the trial that is before us and pray like crazy … until He says, "No." And if no is what He says, we must trust that our loving Father has something greater in mind. Let's remind ourselves through His Word, just how good the Father's plans are for us. Although we've read these passages before, they bear repeating.

10. Read the following passages and respond in a prayer of belief and praise.

Jeremiah 29:10–14

_____

_____

_____

Romans 8:26–28

_____

_____

_____

2 Corinthians 4:13–18

_____

_____

_____

1 Corinthians 2:9–10

_____

_____

_____

_____

As I researched this topic, I came across a myriad of books addressing why God doesn't always answer our prayers. The truth is, my dear friend, He *does* always answer. The trouble for us is that He doesn't always answer the way we want Him to.

I am no theologian or scholar. I'm just a wife with a healed heart who is speaking to another wife whose heart is in the process of healing. I don't have all the answers. In fact, I feel like I have more questions than you probably do. But I am here to tell you that Jesus loves you, God is *for* you, and you can trust Him in *all* things. He *will* answer and bless you in ways you can't now imagine. He will minister to you deeply. No man or earthly circumstance will ever reach the depth of His closeness, which He will draw you into. That alone is worth continuing to pursue Him.

> "Having therefore these promises" (2 Corinthians 7:1). I claim the fulfillment of God's promises, and rightly, but that is only the human side; the Divine side is that through the promises I recognize God's claim on me."[15]

James 4:8 tells us, "Draw near to God and He will draw near to you." So keep at Him, dear one. Keep praying. Keep seeking. Keep hoping. Keep believing. Our Redeemer draws near.

DAY 5: CALLED TO A GREATER GLORY

Many are the afflictions of the righteous, But the Lord delivers [her] out of them all … The Lord redeems the soul of His servants, And none of those who take refuge in Him will be condemned. (Psalm 34:19, 22)

The vision is not a castle in the air, but a vision of what God wants you to be. Let Him put you on His wheel and whirl you as He likes, and as sure as God is God and you are you, you will turn out exactly in accordance with the vision. Don't lose heart in the process. If you have ever had the vision of God, you may try as you like to be satisfied on a lower level, but God will never let you.[46]

When a wounded heart becomes whole and a relationship that was near death is resuscitated and thriving with new life, we see the glory of our King. When a wife who was scared, angry, and bitter becomes a joyful partner, lover, and life giver, others see the glory of the Redeemer. When a husband who was negative, frustrated, and dissatisfied transforms into a gentle, loving, and selfless caregiver, his family shines with redemption and a holy glow.

This is the vision God has laid before us. As Chambers says in the above quote, God intends to mold us into that vision. Try as we may to find gratification in another way (some other form of fulfillment), His Spirit dwelling within us will be restless and unsatisfied until He has worked out all that He has planned. Instead of baulking against Him, seeking our own vision, or pursuing His vision by our own means, we press on. We continue on the path that the Creator has laid out for us. We trust Him to mold us into the form of His vision—the vision of the marriage that He designed and the vision of our healed hearts.

Day after day, week after week, we have sought out, studied, pursued, and prayed for the redemption of our King to become manifest in our lives. We now come to the end of our time together. The call to us is simply to continue believing and keep walking. We must continue with what we have learned. We must keep seeking, praying, dying to ourselves, and trusting Jesus. As each year passes and we are transformed by our continued faith, we will look back and see the incredible, intense glory that has come over us, such that, we will shine with a brightness that is undeniable to those around us.

1. Read Exodus 34:4–10 and 29–35 and respond to what the Spirit speaks to you.

_____

_____

_____

_____

2. What does Moses ask of the Lord in verse 9?

_____

_____

_____

_____

3. How does this relate to you and your circumstance?

_____

_____

_____

_____

4. What is God's response to Moses in verse 10?

_____

_____

_____

_____

5. Does this statement increase your faith that the Lord is committed to completing your healing? Why or why not? Write your response as a prayer to God.

_____

_____

_____

_____

In this scene, we see Moses speaking with the Almighty, spending time in His presence, beholding the very being of the invisible Creator (though he cannot look upon His face), and quite literally absorbing His glory. The immense shine of the King's glory was so intense that Moses's face glowed brightly, and the people were afraid to come near him. How incredible! Can you imagine glowing with the glory of the Lord in such a tangible way that people around you feel uncomfortable? I believe our healed lives do just that. Paul the apostle also believed this. Read of his account in 2 Corinthians 3:13–4:1.

> [We] are not like Moses, who used to put a veil over his face so that the sons of Israel would not look intently at the end of what was fading away. But their minds were hardened; for until this very day at the reading of the old covenant the same veil remains unlifted, because it is removed in Christ. But to this day whenever Moses is read, a veil lies over their heart; but whenever a person turns to the Lord, the veil is taken away. Now the Lord is the Spirit, and where the Spirit of the Lord is, there is liberty. But we all, with unveiled face, beholding as in a mirror the glory of the Lord, are being transformed into the same image from glory to glory, just as from the Lord, the Spirit. Therefore, since we have this ministry, as we received mercy, we do not lose heart.

I absolutely love this: "Therefore, since we have this ministry." We have the ministry of being changed from "glory to glory" by the King of creation. We will be transformed from the glory that we already shine, because of the transformation accomplished when we first believed, to an even greater glory. When we are transformed by each trial as we draw upon the depth of God's riches, we shine more and more brightly with His grace and beauty. Our faces are unveiled.

We have liberty to boldly run to Jesus at *any* time seeking "that we may receive mercy and find grace to help in time of need," as Hebrews 4:16 tells us. Unlike Moses who hid his face and concealed what God had done for him, we speak of His graciousness and power in us. We share the love and mercy that has been made available to us by the blood of Jesus. In that, we shine with His glory. If all that weren't enough, we have the privilege of looking into the unveiled face of the Savior. Seeing His glory as if looking into a mirror, we are able to see our own faces shine back at us.

Our shining with the grace and mercy of the King makes others uncomfortable. They don't quite know what to do with us. They are convicted by our commitment to remain in a damaged marriage. They are confused and astounded by our determination to make intimacy with our husbands a priority. They can't understand how we are able to truly forgive, hold no grudge, and bear no marks of resentment. Their hearts and minds are veiled by their unbelief, but the peculiarity of our lives pricks their spirits and causes them to wonder what is so different about us.

The discomfort of this pricking will hopefully cause them to look for Jesus, and in seeking, we pray that they may find Him. Isn't this the greatest glory of all? We have the honor and privilege of displaying Jesus before a watching world and pointing them to His grace and redemption. What a gift this is!

Paul also says in the previous passage, "Therefore, since we have this ministry, as we received mercy, we do not lose heart" (2 Corinthians 4:1). Since we know that we already possess the power, provision, and shining light of the Holy Spirit within our souls, we can move into the future with joy and hope. We do not loose heart. There is no need for discouragement.

Don't get me wrong. Discouragement, discontentment, and disillusions will try to creep into our minds. The enemy will still attempt to veil our eyes with lies and deception, but we have the ability to cast out all these things and cling to the boundless grace of our Redeemer. We have the promise that Jesus has already overcome it all. Read Revelation 12:10–11 and notice the means by which we overcome the enemy and his lies.

> *Then I heard a loud voice in heaven, saying, "Now the salvation, and the power, and the kingdom of our God and the authority of His Christ have come, for the accuser of our brethren has been thrown down, he who accuses them before our God day and night. And they overcame him because of the blood of the Lamb and because of the word of their testimony, and they did not love their life even when faced with death."*

6. According to this passage, how do we overcome the accusations of the enemy?

By the blood of the Lamb	By loving Jesus more than ourselves even when faced with the death of our own will
By the word of our testimony	All of the above

I know that was a tricky one because I added words to one of the choices that aren't exactly in the text. I hope you were able to read into it all that I did. John said that the *brethren* or *brothers and sisters*, as the New International Version translates it, overcame the enemy because they did not love their lives, even when faced with death. You and I aren't often asked to face death in a physical sense, but we are constantly looking into the death of our own rights, desires, self-will, and pride, aren't we?

It is only by loving Jesus more than ourselves that we are able to overcome the accuser of our souls. When Satan comes in with a flood of accusations against our husbands, memories of the old things, or little criticisms of their present behaviors, we cry out to Jesus, renounce our claim to our own rights, and cling to the testimony of our redeemed marriage. We stand firm in the blood of the Lamb and affirm the truth that the Holy Spirit is still in the process of transforming us—and our husbands.

Let's return now to Moses. Prior to his mountaintop experience with God when he was bold enough to request to see the glory of the Most High, he was a weary, defeated former prince, living in a foreign land as a fugitive and tending his father-in-law's sheep. I have heard it said that God had blessed Moses in the place where he was and that he was content and comfortable. Maybe that is true, but how can one be entirely comfortable with a murder hanging around in the back of one's mind?

Nonetheless, he was content enough not to go looking for a new vision. He had been given a life calling years earlier, attempted to work it out in his own way, and failed miserably. Living in Midian with his wife and new son seemed much safer than seeking to regain the vision and fulfilling his life's call. Read Exodus 3:1–11 to see how God showed up to shake Moses out of his apathy.

7. What is Moses's response to God? How does that reveal the condition of his heart?

_____

_____

_____

8. Prior to your current trial, had you become comfortable, apathetic, or even lazy in your marriage? In what ways was this true?

_____

_____

_____

9. Prior to the struggle to remain married, had God given you a life calling? What was/is it?

_____

_____

_____

10. Had you become lazy and complacent with that calling?

☐ Yes

☐ Maybe

☐ Not at all

Whether we realize it or not, each of us has a calling. Maybe your mother didn't teach you the purpose of your life while you were growing up as Moses's mother probably did. I'm guessing you've never been visited by an angel like Mary was or entertained God Himself as Abraham did, but you have a purpose and a calling nonetheless.

If you are a mother, one of your callings is to raise a godly generation. If you have neighbors, friends, or coworkers who don't know Jesus, your calling is to minister Jesus to them. If you are a wife (which of course you are because you are doing this study), your calling is to be a godly counselor to and supporter of your husband. Though these are simplistic examples of God's purposes for your life, it is not my goal to tell you what the Holy Spirit has planned for you but to remind you that God has given you purpose and influence in every area of your life.

You can stand in any place, and someone will be desperate for the knowledge you possess. There is no circumstance that the King hasn't ordained for you to be a light and a minister of His truth and love in.

11. Do you believe this? I mean do you truly believe this? Why or why not?

_____

_____

_____

_____

Our greatest calling and the very essence of our living and breathing are to display the glory of our King so that those around us may be drawn to Him. As you continue to heal, to draw closer to Jesus, and are reunited to your husband, my earnest prayer is that you will open your heart and life to those around you, shine the glory of God's redemption, and minister the forgiveness of your King to a hurting world.

I pray that you will have the courage to share your story with someone who has also been wounded. Even if it is just one person, think of the lives that will be changed by the ripple effect if you encourage her and she turns to uplift another. Think of the lives of their children and their children's marriages, as they each begin displaying redemption to those around them. God can do an incredible thing with just one changed life.

Marriages all over the world are suffering and people in our circles of influence are lost and broken. I pray that you and I will be the example of Jesus to them in a real and tangible way.

12. Name one marriage that you know of, other than your own, which is suffering this very moment.

_____

_____

_____

_____

13. How can this couple benefit from what God has taught you through these past five weeks?

_____

_____

_____

_____

Our Redeemer has given us a vision of glory, dear one. It is a vision of a healed wife and a redeemed marriage. We have seen His vision of forgiveness, mercy, cleansing, and friendship. His vision for us is joy and fellowship with Himself and our husbands. In all these things, His glory shines through to those around us, making all that we have endured a worthwhile blessing, as we pass the vision on to those around us.

I am so very proud of you for finishing this journey with me. I am deeply humbled and honored to have been part of your healing. As we part ways, I pray that you journey on in faith and courage, fervently pursuing all that the King has prepared for you.

Let us pray one last time together.

Father, King of heaven,

We praise You for Your immense grace, which has covered our every step along this road to healing. We acknowledge that You are not done with us yet. We praise You for how far we've come, and we look to You to be the strength, courage, and peace that we need to move forward into the next leg of our journey. We know that there will be valleys and rocky mountain faces to climb, but we believe and trust You to carry us through every step. We ask that You use our lives and our broken pieces for Your glory, our good, and the good of those around us. May we seek to honor You in every conversation, interaction, and task, every day. In Jesus's name we ask, amen.

The eyes of the Lord are toward the righteous

And His ears are open to their cry.

The face of the Lord is against evildoers,

To cut off the memory of them from the earth.

The righteous cry, and the Lord hears

And delivers them out of all their troubles.

The Lord is near to the brokenhearted

And saves those who are crushed in spirit.

Many are the afflictions of the righteous,

But the Lord delivers him out of them all.

He keeps all his bones,

Not one of them is broken.

Evil shall slay the wicked,

And those who hate the righteous will be condemned.

The Lord redeems the soul of His servants,

And none of those who take refuge in Him will be condemned.

(Psalm 34:15–22)

NOTES

Week 1

1   Oswald Chambers, "June 25" in *My Utmost for His Highest*. (Grand Rapids, Michigan: Discovery House Publishers, 1963).

Day 2

2   D. Guzik, "Study Guide for Job 37," Blue Letter Bible, accessed January 21, 2018, https://www.blueletterbible.org/Comm/guzik_david/StudyGuide2017-Job/Job-37.cfm?a=473003.

Day 3

3   "Emeth," *Lexicon: Strongs* H571, Blue Letter Bible, accessed February 1, 2018, https://www.blueletterbible.org/lang/lexicon/lexicon.cfm?Strongs=H571&t=KJV.

4   *"Amēn,"* *Lexicon: Strongs* G281, Blue Letter Bible, accessed September 16, 2019, https://www.blueletterbible.org/lang/lexicon/lexicon.cfm?Strongs=G281&t=KJV.

Day 4

5   Chambers, "August 25" in *My Utmost*.

6   Matt Redman, J. Ingram, "Never Once," *10,000 Reasons* (M. Redman, T. Wanstall, sixstepsrecords/ Sparrow Records, July 2011).

7   *"Dynastēs,"* *Lexicon: Strongs* G1413, Blue Letter Bible, accessed January 18, 2019, https://www.blueletterbible.org/lang/lexicon/lexicon.cfm?Strongs=G1413&t=KJV.

8   Ibid.

9   Guzik, "Study Guide for 1 Timothy 6," Blue Letter Bible, accessed January 29, 2018, https://www.blueletterbible.org/Comm/guzik_david/StudyGuide2017-1Ti/1Ti-6.cfm?a=1125004.

Day 5

10   Chambers, "August 10" in *My Utmost*.

Week 2

Day 1

11   K. Scott, "At the Foot of the Cross (Ashes To Beauty)," *Satisfy* (Integrity Worship Music, ASCAP, 2003).

Day 2

12 *"`Ezer," Lexicon: Strongs* H5828, Blue Letter Bible, accessed June 1, 2018, https://www.blueletterbible.org/lang/lexicon/lexicon.cfm?Strongs=H5828&t=KJV.

13 John Eldridge, "Eve is Essential," Wild at Heart, accessed January 2, 2021, https://wildatheart.org/daily-reading/eve-essential.

14 *"Kanaph," Lexicon: Strongs* H3671, Blue Letter Bible, accessed June 1, 2018, https://www.blueletterbible.org/lang/lexicon/lexicon.cfm?Strongs=H3671&t=KJV.

15 D. Guzik, "Study Guide for Malachi 2," Blue Letter Bible, accessed Febraury 1, 2018, https://www.blueletterbible.org/Comm/guzik_david/StudyGuide2017-Mal/Mal-2.cfm?a=927002.

16 Ibid.

17 Ibid.

18 *"Chamac," Lexicon: Strongs* H2555, Blue Letter Bible, accessed June 1, 2018, https://www.blueletterbible.org/lang/lexicon/lexicon.cfm?Strongs=H2555&t=KJV.

19 A.R. Fausset, *Jamieson, Fausset & Brown: Commentary on Malachi 2*, Blue Letter Bible, accessed February 1, 2019, https://www.blueletterbible.org/Comm/jfb/Mal/Mal_002.cfm?a=927002.

20 W. MacDonald, *Believer's Bible Commentary: Old Testament* (Nashville, Tennessee: Thomas Nelson, Inc., 1990), 1175.

21 *"Chamac," Lexicon: Strongs* H2555.

Day 5

22 Chambers, "May 23" in *My Utmost.*

23 K. Grant, *The Keys to His Kingdom: Praying in the Word of God* (Greenwood Village, Colorado: The Bread of Life Foundation, 1995).

24 *"Pistis," Lexicon: Strongs* G4102, Blue Letter Bible, accessed June 9, 2018, https://www.blueletterbible.org/lang/lexicon/lexicon.cfm?Strongs=G4102&t=KJV.

25 *Prayer Quotes – Oswald Chambers*, Prayer Coach, accessed September 23, 2019, https://prayer-coach.com/2011/06/10/prayer-quotes-oswald-chambers/.

Week 3

Day 1

26 Hillsong Church, "Forever Reign," *A Beautiful Exchange* (J. Ingram, R. Morgan, Hillsong Music Australia, 2010).

Day 2

27 H. Cloud, J. Townsend, *Boundaries in Marriage* (Grand Rapids, Michigan: Zondervan, 2002).

Day 3

28 Chambers, "February 17" in *My Utmost.*

Week 4

Day 1

29 *"Yare'," Lexicon: Strongs* H3373, Blue Letter Bible, accessed October 1, 2019, https://www.blueletterbible.org/lang/lexicon/lexicon.cfm?Strongs=H3373&t=KJV.

30 *"Yir'ah," Lexicon: Strongs* H3374, Blue Letter Bible, accessed October 1, 2019, https://www.blueletterbible.org/lang/lexicon/lexicon.cfm?Strongs=H3374&t=KJV.

31 Chambers, "August 25" in *My Utmost*.

Day 2

32 Chambers, "February 7" in *My Utmost*.

Day 3

33 "Hypocrisy," *Merriam-Webster*, Inc., accessed August 10, 2018, https://www.merriam-webster.com/dictionary/hypocrisy.

Day 4

34 J. Williams, sermon April 22, 2018, Westside Community Church, El Paso, Texas.

Day 5

35 "What Is Forgiveness?" The Greater Good Science Center at the University of California, Berkeley, accessed January 21, 2019, https://greatergood.berkeley.edu/topic/forgiveness/definition.

36 "What is Forgiveness?" Got Questions Ministries, accessed January 29, 2019, https://www.gotquestions.org/what-is-forgiveness.html.

37 Ibid.

38 "What Is Forgiveness?" The Greater Good Science Center.

Week 5

Day 1

39 *"Kaphar," Lexicon: Strongs* H3722, Blue Letter Bible, accessed October 20, 2019, https://www.blueletterbible.org/lang/lexicon/lexicon.cfm?Strongs=H3722&t=KJV.

40 Chambers, "December 13" in *My Utmost*.

41 D. Guzik, "Study Guide for Ephesians 1," Blue Letter Bible, accessed February 10, 2019, https://www.blueletterbible.org/Comm/guzik_david/StudyGuide2017-Eph/Eph-1.cfm?a=1098002.

42 Ibid.

Day 3

43 Elevation Worship, "Do it Again," *There Is a Cloud* (C. Brown, M. Brock, M. Redman, S. Furtick, Elevation Worship Records, February 2017).

44 "Definition of communion in English," *Oxford Dictionary*, Lexico.com, accessed March 10, 2019, https://www.lexico.com/en/definition/communion.

Day 4

45 Chambers, "March 18" in *My Utmost*.

Day 5

46 Chambers, "July 6" in *My Utmost*.

RECOMMENDED RESOURCES

Boundaries in Marriage by Dr. Henry Cloud and Dr. John Townsend
Captivating by John and Stasi Eldredge
Fearless by Eric Blehm
Love & Respect by Dr. Emerson Eggerichs
Praying in the Word of God: Advancing Christ's Kingdom by Kathleen G. Grant
Rocking the Roles by Robert Lewis and William Hendricks
SOS: Sick of Sex by Robyn McKelvy
Swipe Right by Levi Lusko
The New Eve: Choosing God's Best for Your Life by Robert Lewis
When You've Been Wronged: Moving From Bitterness to Forgiveness by Erwin W.Lutzer
Why Godly People Do Ungodly Things: Arming Yourself in the Age of Seduction by Beth Moore
Why Us?: When Bad Things Happen to God's People by Warren Wiersbe
Wild at Heart: Discovering the Secret of a Mans's Soul by John Eldredge
You and Me Forever: Marriage in Light of Eternity by Francis and Lisa Chan

Printed in the United States
by Baker & Taylor Publisher Services